Grades 2–3

Reading & Writing
LESSONS FOR THE SMART BOARD™

Motivating, Interactive Lessons That Teach Key Reading & Writing Skills

■ SCHOLASTIC

New York ○ Toronto ○ London ○ Auckland ○ Sydney
New Delhi ○ Mexico City ○ Hong Kong ○ Buenos Aires

Teaching *Resources*

Authors: Karen Mawer (Gr. 2), Eileen Jones (Gr. 3)
Illustrators: Jim Peacock (Notebook file illustrations), Mark Brierley (Notebook file and book illustrations), Theresa Tibbetts (additional Notebook file illustrations), Andy Keylock (book illustrations), Chris Saunderson (additional Notebook file illustrations), Ian Hunt (additional book illustrations)
Editor: Maria L. Chang
Cover design: Brian LaRossa
Interior design: Grafica Inc.

CD-ROM developed in association with Q & D Multimedia

Special thanks to Robin Hunt and Melissa Rugless of Scholastic Ltd.

SMART Board™ and Notebook™ are registered trademarks of SMART Technologies Inc.

Microsoft Office, Word, and Excel are either registered trademarks or trademarks of Microsoft Corporation in the United States and/or other countries.

All Flash activities designed and developed by Q & D Multimedia.

Contents

Introduction

Interactive whiteboards are fast becoming the must-have resource in today's classroom as they allow teachers to facilitate children's learning in ways that were inconceivable a few years ago. The appropriate use of interactive whiteboards, whether used daily in the classroom or once a week in a computer lab, encourages active participation in lessons and increases students' determination to succeed. Interactive whiteboards make it easier for teachers to bring subjects across the curriculum to life in new and exciting ways.

What can an interactive whiteboard offer?

For teachers, an interactive whiteboard allows them to do the same things they can on an ordinary whiteboard, such as drawing, writing, and erasing. However, the interactive whiteboard also offers many other possibilities, such as:

- saving any work created during a lesson;
- preparing as many pages as necessary;
- displaying any page within the Notebook™ file to review teaching and learning;
- adding scanned examples of the children's work to a Notebook file;
- changing colors of shapes and backgrounds instantly;
- using simple templates and grids;
- linking Notebook files to spreadsheets, Web sites, and presentations.

Using an interactive whiteboard in the simple ways outlined above can enrich teaching and learning in a classroom, but that is only the beginning of the whiteboard's potential to educate and inspire.

For students, the interactive whiteboard provides the opportunity to share learning experiences, as lessons can be delivered with sound, still and moving images, and Web sites. Interactive whiteboards can be used to cater to the needs of all learning styles:

- Kinesthetic learners benefit from being able to physically manipulate images.
- Visual learners benefit from being able to watch videos, look at photographs, and see images being manipulated.
- Auditory learners benefit from being able to access audio resources, such as voice recordings and sound effects.

With a little preparation, all of these resource types could be integrated into one lesson—a feat that would have been almost impossible before the advent of the interactive whiteboard!

Access to an interactive whiteboard

In schools where students have limited access to an interactive whiteboard, carefully planned lessons will help students get the most benefit from it during the times they can use it. As teachers become familiar with the interactive whiteboard, they will learn when to use it and, equally important, when not to use it!

Where permanent access to an interactive whiteboard is available, it is important to plan the use of the board effectively. It should be used only in ways that will enhance or extend teaching and learning. Children still need to gain practical, first-hand experience of many things. Some experiences cannot be recreated on an interactive whiteboard, but others cannot be had without it. *Reading & Writing Lessons for the SMART Board*™ offers both teachers and learners the most accessible and creative uses of this most valuable resource.

About the book

Adapted from Scholastic UK's best-selling 100 SMART Board™ Lessons series, *Reading & Writing Lessons for the SMART Board*™ is designed to reflect best practice in using interactive whiteboards. It is also designed to support all teachers in using this valuable tool by providing lessons and other resources that can be used on the SMART Board with little or no preparation. These inspirational lessons meet the English language arts Common Core State Standards and are perfect for all levels of experience.

This book is divided into three chapters. Each chapter contains lessons covering:

- Reading, Spelling & Vocabulary
- Writing
- Grammar, Mechanics & Usage

Mini-Lessons

The mini-lessons have a consistent structure that includes:

- a **Getting Started** activity;
- a step-by-step **Mini-Lesson** plan;
- an **Independent Work** activity; and
- a **Wrap-Up** activity to round up the teaching and learning and identify any assessment opportunities.

Each mini-lesson identifies any resources required (including Notebook files that are provided on the CD-ROM, as well as reproducible activity pages) and lists the whiteboard tools that could be used in the mini-lesson.

The reproducible activity sheets toward the back of the book support the mini-lessons. These sheets provide opportunities for group or individual work to be completed away from the board, while linking to the context of the whiteboard lesson. They also provide opportunities for whole-class discussions in which children present their work.

What's on the CD-ROM?

The accompanying CD-ROM provides an extensive bank of Notebook files designed for use with the SMART Board. These support, and are supported by, the mini-lessons in this book. They can be annotated and saved for reference or for use with subsequent lessons; they can also be printed out. In addition to texts and images, a selection of Notebook files include the following types of files:

- **Embedded Microsoft Word files:** The embedded files are launched from the Notebook file and will open in their native Microsoft application.
- **Embedded interactive files:** These include specially commissioned interactive files that will open in a new browser window within the Notebook environment.
- **Embedded audio files:** Some Notebook files contain buttons that play sounds.
- **"Build Your Own" file:** This contains a blank Notebook page with a bank of selected images and interactive tools from the Gallery, as well as specially commissioned images. It is supported by the mini-lesson plans in the book to help you build your own Notebook files.

The Notebook files

All of the Notebook files have a consistent structure as follows:

- **Title and objectives page**—Use this page to highlight the focus of the mini-lesson. You might also wish to refer to this page at certain times throughout the lesson or at the end of the lesson to assess whether the learning objective was achieved.
- **Getting Started activity**—This sets the context to the lesson and usually provides some key questions or learning points that will be addressed through the main activities.
- **Main activities**—These activities offer independent, collaborative group, or whole-class work. The activities draw on the full scope of Notebook software and the associated tools, as well as the SMART Board tools. "What to Do" boxes are also included in many of the prepared Notebook files. These appear as tabs in the top right-hand corner of the screen. To access these notes, simply pull out the tabs to reveal planning information, additional support, and key learning points.
- **Wrap-Up**—A whole-class activity or summary page is designed to review work done both at the board and away from the board. In many lessons, children are encouraged to present their work.

How to Use the CD-ROM

Setting up your screen for optimal use

It is best to view the Notebook pages at a screen display setting of 1280 x 1024 pixels. To alter the screen display, select Settings, then Control Panel from the Start menu. Next, double-click on the Display icon, then click on the Settings tab. Finally, adjust the Screen area scroll bar to 1280 x 1024 pixels. Click on OK. (On the Mac, click on the apple icon and select System Preferences. Then click on Displays and select 1280 x 1024.)

If you prefer to use a screen display setting of 800 x 600 pixels, ensure that your Notebook view is set to "Page Width." To alter the view, launch Notebook and click on View. Go to Zoom and select the "Page Width" setting. If you use a screen display setting of 800 x 600 pixels, text in the prepared Notebook files may appear larger when you edit it on screen.

Getting started

The program should run automatically when you insert the CD-ROM into your CD drive. If it does not, use My Computer to browse to the contents of the CD-ROM and click on the Scholastic icon. (On the Mac, click on the Scholastic icon to start the program.)

Main menu

The Main menu divides the Notebook files by topic: Reading, Spelling & Vocabulary; Writing; and Grammar, Mechanics & Usage. Clicking on the appropriate button for any of these options will take you to a separate Lessons menu. (See below for further information.) The "Build Your Own" file is also accessed through the Main menu.

Individual Notebook files or pages can be located using the search facility by keying in words (or part of words) from the resource titles in the Search box. Press Go to begin the search. This will bring up a list of the titles that match your search.

Lessons menu

Each Lessons menu provides all of the prepared Notebook files for each chapter of the book. Click on the buttons to open the Notebook files. Click on Main menu button to return to the Main menu screen. (To alternate between the menus on the CD-ROM and other open applications, hold down the Alt key and press the Tab key to switch to the desired application.)

"Build Your Own" file

Click on this button to open a blank Notebook page and a collection of Gallery objects, which will be saved automatically into the My Content folder in the Gallery. (Under My Content, open the Year 3 Folder, then the English folder to access the Gallery objects.) You only need to click on this button the first time you wish to access the "Build Your Own" file, as the Gallery objects will remain in the My Content folder on the computer on which the file was opened. To use the facility again, simply open a blank Notebook page and access the images and interactive resources from the same folder under My Content. If you are using the CD-ROM on a different computer, you will need to click on the "Build Your Own" button again.

Safety note: Avoid looking directly at the projector beam as it is potentially damaging to the eyes, and never leave children unsupervised when using the interactive whiteboard.

Connections to the Common Core State Standards

The mini-lessons and activities in this book meet the following Common Core State Standards for English Language Arts:

READING, SPELLING & VOCABULARY	
Long-Vowel Sounds	**RF.2.3a:** Distinguish long and short vowels when reading regularly spelled one-syllable words.
/oi/ Vowel Sound	**RF.2.3b:** Know spelling-sound correspondences for additional common vowel teams.
/ou/ Vowel Sound	**RF.2.3b:** Know spelling-sound correspondences for additional common vowel teams.
/âr/ Vowel Sound	**RF.2.3b:** Know spelling-sound correspondences for additional common vowel teams. **RF.2.3e:** Identify words with inconsistent but common spelling-sound correspondences. **RF.2.3f:** Recognize and read grade-appropriate irregularly spelled words.
/ûr/ Vowel Sound	**RF.2.3b:** Know spelling-sound correspondences for additional common vowel teams. **RF.2.3e:** Identify words with inconsistent but common spelling-sound correspondences. **RF.2.3f:** Recognize and read grade-appropriate irregularly spelled words.
Broad /ô/ Vowel Sound	**RF.2.3b:** Know spelling-sound correspondences for additional common vowel teams. **RF.2.3e:** Identify words with inconsistent but common spelling-sound correspondences. **RF.2.3f:** Recognize and read grade-appropriate irregularly spelled words.
Words Ending in -le	**RF.2.3e:** Identify words with inconsistent but common spelling-sound correspondences. **RF.2.3f:** Recognize and read grade-appropriate irregularly spelled words.
Prefixes un- and dis-	**RF.2.3d:** Decode words with common prefixes and suffixes. **RF.3.3a:** Identify and know the meaning of the most common prefixes and derivational suffixes. **RF.3.3c:** Decode multisyllable words. **RF.3.3d:** Read grade-appropriate irregularly spelled words. **L.2.4b:** Determine the meaning of the new word formed when a known prefix is added to a known word.
Suffixes -ful and -ly	**RF.2.3d:** Decode words with common prefixes and suffixes. **RF.3.3a:** Identify and know the meaning of the most common prefixes and derivational suffixes. **RF.3.3c:** Decode multisyllable words. **RF.3.3d:** Read grade-appropriate irregularly spelled words. **L.3.4b:** Determine the meaning of the new word formed when a known affix is added to a known word.
Antonyms	n/a

Synonyms	**L.2.4e:** Use glossaries and beginning dictionaries, both print and digital, to determine or clarify the meaning of words and phrases.
Homonyms	**L.2.4a and L.3.4a:** Use sentence-level context as a clue to the meaning of a word or phrase.
Compound Words	**L.2.4d:** Use knowledge of the meaning of individual words to predict the meaning of compound words.
Words Within Words	**L.3.2f:** Use spelling patterns and generalizations (e.g., meaningful word parts) in writing words.
Alphabetical Order	n/a

WRITING

Firework Poem	**RL.2.4:** Describe how words and phrases supply rhythm and meaning in a story, poem, or song.
Organizing Ideas	**RI.2.7:** Explain how specific images contribute to and clarify a text. **W.3.2a:** Introduce a topic and group related information together; include illustrations when useful to aiding comprehension.
Following Directions	**RI.2.7:** Explain how specific images contribute to and clarify a text. **W.3.2a:** Introduce a topic and group related information together; include illustrations when useful to aiding comprehension.
Retelling an Event	**W.2.3:** Write narratives in which they recount a well-elaborated event or short sequence of events. **SL.2.4:** Tell a story or recount an experience with appropriate facts and relevant, descriptive details, speaking audibly in coherent sentences.
Time Signals	**W.2.3:** Write narratives in which they recount a well-elaborated event or short sequence of events, including use temporal words to signal event order. **W.3.3c:** Use temporal words and phrases to signal event order.
Story Setting	**W.3.3:** Write narratives to develop real or imagined experiences or events using effective technique, descriptive details, and clear event sequences.
Setting and Atmosphere	**W.3.3:** Write narratives to develop real or imagined experiences or events using effective technique, descriptive details, and clear event sequences.
Character Profiles	**W.3.3a:** Establish a situation and introduce a narrator and/or characters.
Narrative and Dialogue	**W.2.3:** Write narratives in which they recount a well-elaborated event or short sequence of events, include details to describe actions, thoughts, and feelings. **W.3.3b:** Use dialogue and descriptions of actions, thoughts, and feelings to develop experiences and events or show the response of characters to situations.
Perspective and Character	**W.2.3:** Write narratives in which they recount a well-elaborated event or short sequence of events, include details to describe actions, thoughts, and feelings. **W.3.3b:** Use dialogue and descriptions of actions, thoughts, and feelings to develop experiences and events or show the response of characters to situations.

Story Planning in Paragraphs	**W.2.3:** Write narratives in which they recount a well-elaborated event or short sequence of events.
Creating a Storyboard	**W.2.3:** Write narratives in which they recount a well-elaborated event or short sequence of events.
Story Planning	**W.2.3:** Write narratives in which they recount a well-elaborated event or short sequence of events.
Editing Unnecessary Words	**L.3.3a:** Choose words and phrases for effect. **L.3.3b:** Recognize and observe differences between the conventions of spoken and written standard English.

GRAMMAR, MECHANICS & USAGE

Sentences	**L.2.1f:** Produce, expand, and rearrange complete simple and compound sentences.
Verbs	**L.3.1a:** Explain the function of verbs in general and their function in particular sentences. **L.3.1e:** Form and use the simple verb tenses. **L.3.2e:** Use conventional spelling for high-frequency and other studied words and for adding suffixes to base words.
Words Ending in -ed	**L.3.2e:** Use conventional spelling for high-frequency and other studied words and for adding suffixes to base words.
Past, Present & Future Tenses	**L.2.1d:** Form and use the past tense of frequently occurring irregular verbs. **L.3.1e:** Form and use the simple verb tenses.
Adjectives	**L.2.1e:** Use adjectives and adverbs, and choose between them depending on what is to be modified.
Singular & Plural Nouns	**L.2.1b:** Form and use frequently occurring irregular plural nouns. **L.3.1b:** Form and use regular and irregular plural nouns.
Conjunctions	**L.3.1h:** Use coordinating and subordinating conjunctions. **W.3.2c:** Use linking words and phrases to connect ideas within categories of information
Capitalization & Periods	**L.2.2 and L.3.2:** Demonstrate command of the conventions of standard English capitalization, punctuation, and spelling when writing.
Question Marks	**L.2.2 and L.3.2:** Demonstrate command of the conventions of standard English capitalization, punctuation, and spelling when writing.
Commas	**L.2.2 and L.3.2:** Demonstrate command of the conventions of standard English capitalization, punctuation, and spelling when writing.
Quotation Marks	**L.3.2c:** Use commas and quotation marks in dialogue.
Punctuating Dialogue	**L.3.2c:** Use commas and quotation marks in dialogue.
Apostrophes & Contractions	**L.2.2c:** Use an apostrophe to form contractions and frequently occurring possessives.

Long-Vowel Sounds

Learning objective
- To spell with increasing accuracy and confidence, drawing on word recognition, knowledge of word structure, and spelling patterns, including common inflections and use of double letters.

Resources
- "Long-Vowel Sounds" Notebook file
- "Long-Vowel Sounds" (p. 53)
- a shared text containing several examples of long-vowel sounds
- individual whiteboards and pens
- prepared chart divided in five sections (see Independent Work)

Whiteboard tools
- Eraser
- Pen tray
- Spotlight tool
- Select tool
- Highlighter pen
- On-screen Keyboard
- Screen Shade

Getting Started

Open the "Long-Vowel Sounds" Notebook file and display page 2. Remind students of the five long-vowel sounds and give some quick examples of some words that contain them.

Read a shared text together (see Resources). Ask students to listen for words containing a long-vowel sound. Invite them to touch their nose every time they think they hear a word containing a long-vowel sound.

Mini-Lesson

1. Invite students to look at the long-vowel sound at the top of each box on page 3 of the Notebook file. Encourage them to think of ways to spell these long-vowel sounds and to discuss ideas with a partner.

2. Take the cards out of the box one at a time. Invite students to decide what sound each one makes, then drag the cards into the correct boxes.

3. Using the word wall on page 4, ask students to read each word. Use the Spotlight tool to focus on one word at a time.

4. Pick out the long-vowel sound in each word, emphasizing the sound it makes within the word. Invite volunteers to come to the SMART Board to highlight the long-vowel sounds.

5. Sound out some of the words as examples.

6. Provide students with individual whiteboards and, using page 5, which shows pictures of objects whose names contain a long-vowel sound, challenge students to spell the words. Invite individuals to use a Pen from the Pen tray to write the words into the boxes beneath the pictures. Then reveal the correct answers by using the Eraser to rub over the area below each white box.

Independent Work

Divide the class into small groups. Give each group a set of cards prepared from "Long-Vowel Sounds" (p. 53) and a chart divided into five sections—one for each long-vowel sound. Ask students to work together to sort the cards into five groups according to the long-vowel sound they contain. Encourage students to insert the correct spelling of the sound into the words. Then have them write the words into the correct column of the chart. Challenge them to think of more words to add to their tables, or to put the words they have sorted into sentences.

Supply less-confident learners with cards that contain only one spelling of each vowel sound so that they only have to decide which long-vowel sound to use, and not which spelling.

Wrap-Up

Read more of the shared text with students. Ask them to listen for any words containing a long-vowel sound. Ask students to write these on page 6 of the Notebook file and highlight the long-vowel sounds. Remove all but five words, then hide the page with the Screen Shade and ask students to write them on individual whiteboards. Reveal the board again to check spellings.

/oi/ Vowel Sound

Learning objective

- To spell with increasing accuracy and confidence, drawing on word recognition, knowledge of word structure, and spelling patterns, including common inflections and use of double letters.

Resources

- "/oi/ Vowel Sound" Notebook file
- "Joyful Word Search" (p. 54)
- shared text containing examples of the /oi/ sound
- individual whiteboards and pens

Whiteboard tools

- Pen tray
- Select tool
- On-screen Keyboard
- Spotlight tool
- Highlighter pen

Getting Started

Open the "/oi/ Vowel Sounds" Notebook file and display page 2. Introduce the /oi/ sound to students and give some quick examples of words that contain it, such as *boy*, *voice*, and *oil*.

Ask students to listen for words containing the /oi/ sound as you read the shared text (see Resources) together with the class. Tell them to touch their nose every time they think they hear a word containing the vowel sound.

Mini-Lesson

1. Go to page 3 of the Notebook file and look at the two spellings of the /oi/ sound.

2. In pairs, ask students to think of five words containing the /oi/ sound. Have them list them on their individual whiteboards.

3. Sort the pictures of the /oi/ sound words on page 3 onto either the *oy* or *oi* spelling tower by dragging and dropping them. (The pictures are: *oil*, *toy*, *coins*, and *boy*.)

4. Challenge students to write each word on their individual whiteboards as they are sorted. Emphasize the spelling pattern used.

5. Invite students to share examples of words with the /oi/ sound and add them to the tower.

6. Read all of the words on page 4 and ask students to highlight the words that contain an /oi/ sound. Focus on individual words with the Spotlight tool.

7. Ask students to sort the words into *oy* or *oi* spellings on their individual whiteboards.

Independent Work

Give each student a copy of "Joyful Word Search" (p. 54). Ask students to find ten words that contain an /oi/ sound. The words are written either left to right or top to bottom. Ensure that students list the words on the right-hand side of the page as they locate them. Encourage them to look for places where *oi* and *oy* are together and then see if there is a word around them.

Provide less-confident learners with a list of words to look for. Challenge students who manage to find all ten words to put the words into sentences. Encourage them to check that they are spelling the words correctly when using them in sentences.

Wrap-Up

Return to the Notebook file and complete the crossword on page 5. Ask students to read the clues and think of an answer. Explain that all of the answers will be words that contain the /oi/ sound. Tell students to write their answers on their individual whiteboards, thinking carefully about the spelling of the words. Invite volunteers to complete each answer by dragging the appropriate letters into the boxes. Check the answers by pressing the red answer button.

/ou/ Vowel Sound

Learning objective

- To spell with increasing accuracy and confidence, drawing on word recognition, knowledge of word structure, and spelling patterns, including common inflections and use of double letters.

Resources

- "/ou/ Vowel Sound" Notebook file
- a shared text containing examples of the /ou/ sound
- "Write Out the /ou/ Words" (p. 55)
- individual whiteboards and pens

Whiteboard tools

- Pen tray
- Select tool
- On-screen Keyboard
- Spotlight tool
- Highlighter pen

Getting Started

Open the "/ou/ Vowel Sound" Notebook file and display page 2. Introduce the /ou/ sound to students and give some quick examples of words that contain it, such as *house*, *clown*, and *out*.

Ask students to listen for words containing the /ou/ sound when reading the shared text (see Resources) together. Invite them to touch their nose every time they think they hear a word containing the vowel sound.

Mini-Lesson

1. Go to page 3 of the Notebook file and look at the two spellings of the /ou/ sound.

2. Working in pairs, challenge students to think of five words containing the /ou/ sound. Ask them to list them on their individual whiteboards.

3. Sort the pictures of the /ou/ sound words into either the *ow* or *ou* box on page 3. This could be done using voting methods. Drag and drop the pictures into the correct boxes.

4. Challenge students to write each word as they are sorted and emphasize the spelling pattern used.

5. Invite students to share examples of words with the /ou/ sound. Add these to the appropriate /ou/ spelling box.

6. Read all of the words on page 4. Use the Spotlight tool to focus on one word at a time and then ask students to highlight the words that contain the /ou/ sound.

7. Ask students to sort the words into *ow* or *ou* spellings on their individual whiteboards.

Independent Work

Pair up students and give each pair a copy of "Write Out the /ou/ Words" (p. 55). Tell students that a word containing the /ou/ sound has been omitted from each sentence and replaced with a blank. Have each pair decide which word has been omitted and then fill in the blanks. Regularly remind students that the missing words all contain the /ou/ sound.

Supply less-confident learners with a list of possible words to be placed in the blanks, or supply them with the initial sound for the missing word on the card. (Answers: 1. mouse, 2. Ouch, 3. flour, 4. How, 5. clown, 6. owl, 7. pounds, 8. cow, 9. clouds, 10. towel)

Wrap-Up

Return to the Notebook file and complete the word search on page 5. Ask students to look for words containing the /ou/ sound in the word search. Explain that there are six words altogether. Tell students to write the words they find on their individual whiteboards, copying the spelling of the word carefully. Once they have done this, invite individuals to come to the whiteboard and highlight the words, then write them in the white boxes on the right-hand side of the page. Finally, reveal the correct answers by pulling the tab across from the left-hand side of the page.

/âr/ Vowel Sound

Learning objective

- To spell with increasing accuracy and confidence, drawing on word recognition, knowledge of word structure, and spelling patterns, including common inflections and use of double letters.

Resources

- "/âr/ Vowel Sound" Notebook file
- "Spelling /âr/ Words" (p. 56), copied onto cardstock and cut apart
- shared text containing examples of the /âr/ sound
- individual whiteboards and pens
- pencils
- paper
- large sign for each spelling (see Wrap-Up)

Whiteboard tools

- Eraser
- Pen tray
- Select tool

Getting Started

Display page 2 of the "/âr/ Vowel Sound" Notebook file. Introduce the /âr/ vowel sound to students and give some quick examples of words that contain it, such as *bear*, *care*, and *pair*.

Read the shared text (see Resources) together and ask students to listen for words containing the /âr/ sound as they read. Tell them to touch their nose every time they think they hear a word containing the sound.

Mini-Lesson

1. Ask students to think of all the ways that the /âr/ sound can be spelled (*air*, *ere*, *ear*, *are*) and write these on page 2 of the Notebook file.

2. Read the sentence on page 3. Ask students to look carefully at each spelling of the word *bear*. Explain that each word sounds the same but only one is correct.

3. Ask students to discuss with a partner which spelling is correct. Invite a volunteer to come to the board and press on a word to check the answer. This will produce a cheer or a groan, depending on whether the student is right or wrong. Alternatively, use the Eraser to rub over the space to reveal the missing word in the sentence.

4. Repeat this activity on pages 4 to 7.

5. Have students work in pairs. Using page 8, read out the crossword clues, one at a time. Ask students to write down their answers on their individual whiteboards, considering the spellings carefully.

6. Each time, invite a different student to place the answer into the crossword grid by dragging the letters from the bottom of the page and dropping them into the appropriate positions in the grid.

7. Repeat this until the crossword is completed.

Independent Work

Divide the class into small groups. Give each group a set of word cards prepared from page 56. Ask students to work together as a group to sort the cards into two piles: words that are spelled correctly and words that are spelled incorrectly. Encourage students to discuss choices and work out any disagreements as a group. Allow them time to list the correctly spelled words into a table and then ask them to put the words into sentences. Give students regular reminders to check that they have spelled the words containing the /âr/ sound correctly. Challenge more-confident learners to think of other words containing the /âr/ sound.

Wrap-Up

Go into the hall and place a large sign displaying one of the spellings of the /âr/ sound (*air*, *ere*, *ear*, *are*) on each wall. Ask students to move around the hall quietly and when you say a word, choose which spelling of the /âr/ sound the word contains by moving to the wall displaying that spelling. Use this game as an opportunity to assess which students are making correct, independent decisions and which require more teaching in this area.

/ûr/ Vowel Sound

Learning objective

- To spell with increasing accuracy and confidence, drawing on word recognition, knowledge of word structure, and spelling patterns, including common inflections and use of double letters.

Resources

- "/ûr/ Vowel Sound" Notebook file
- "First Crossword" (p. 57)
- a shared text containing examples of the /ûr/ sound
- prepared 4" x 6" index cards with single letters on each that can be arranged to spell a word containing an /ûr/ sound
- individual whiteboards and pens
- dictionaries

Whiteboard tools

- Eraser
- Pen tray
- Select tool
- Spotlight tool
- Highlighter pen

Getting Started

Open the "/ûr/ Vowel Sound" Notebook file and display page 2. Introduce the /ûr/ vowel sound to students and give some quick examples of words that contain it, such as *bird*, *her*, and *nurse*.

Ask students to listen for words containing the /ûr/ sound when reading the shared text (see Resources) together. Tell them to touch their nose every time they think they hear a word containing the sound.

Mini-Lesson

1. Look at the three different ways to write the /ûr/ sound on page 3 of the Notebook file.

2. Read the sentence on page 3 with students and ask them to decide, with a partner, which spelling of the /ûr/ sound is the correct one to fill the blank in the word.

3. Allow a student to press on the yellow box of their choice on the SMART Board to see if their answer is correct. They will hear a cheer or a groan, depending on whether their choice was right or wrong.

4. When they have found the correct answer, they can either drag the red box into the word or use the Eraser to check the answer.

5. Complete the challenges on pages 4 to 8 in the same way.

6. Using the word wall on page 9, ask students to read each word as you focus on a word at a time with the Spotlight tool.

7. Then look at the whole wall and invite a different student each time to highlight the /ûr/ sound in each word.

8. Go to page 10 and challenge students to spell words containing the /ûr/ sound correctly on their individual whiteboards. Allow some students to use a Pen from the Pen tray to write the words into the boxes beneath the pictures.

9. Once they have done this, use the Eraser to reveal the correct answers beneath each box.

Independent Work

Give each similar-ability pair of students a copy of "First Crossword" (p. 57) to work on together. Remind students that all of the answers will contain the /ûr/ sound. Show them how to use a dictionary to check the spelling of a word if they are unsure of it.

Fill in the initial letter of each clue to help support less-confident learners. Supply more-confident learners with graphing paper and challenge them to make their own /ûr/ sound crossword for a friend.

Wrap-Up

Give each group a set of prepared cards (see Resources) and ask them to arrange the cards so that they spell out a word containing the /ûr/ vowel sound. Tell them to hold up their cards so that the other groups can check the spelling of the word. Discuss any misconceptions or errors. Give each group a list of five anagrams of words containing the /ûr/ sound to solve. Remind students to look for the /ûr/ sound first to give them a clue.

Broad /ô/ Vowel Sound

Learning objective

- To spell with increasing accuracy and confidence, drawing on word recognition, knowledge of word structure, and spelling patterns, including common inflections and use of double letters.

Resources

- "Broad /ô/ Vowel Sound" Notebook file
- "Sort the Broad /ô/ Words" (p. 58), cut apart
- a shared text containing the broad /ô/ sound
- individual whiteboards and pens
- dictionaries
- pencils
- paper

Whiteboard tools

- Pen tray
- Select tool
- Highlighter pen

Getting Started

Open the "Broad /ô/ Vowel Sound" Notebook file and display page 2. Introduce the broad /ô/ vowel sound to students and give some quick examples of words that contain it, such as *door*, *store*, and *taught*.

Ask students to listen for words containing the broad /ô/ vowel sound when reading the shared text together. Tell them to touch their nose every time they think they hear a word containing the vowel sound.

Mini-Lesson

1. Look at the five different ways to write the broad /ô/ vowel sound on page 3 of the Notebook file.

2. Drag a card from the Words box and ask a student to read the word. Ask students to decide which spelling of the broad /ô/ sound the word belongs to and then invite an individual to drag the word into the correct place.

3. Once all of the cards have been sorted, challenge students, in pairs, to think of three more words containing the broad /ô/ sound. Supply individual whiteboards so that students can record their suggestions. Discuss how to spell the words.

4. Show students a dictionary and ask them what it can be used for. Explain how to locate a word in a dictionary. Look up the meaning of some of the words on the SMART Board.

5. Challenge a few students to locate words in a dictionary. Ask them to explain to the class what they did to find the word.

Independent Work

Give each group a set of "Sort the Broad /ô/ Words" cards (p. 58). Ask students to sort out the words that contain the broad /ô/ sound and make sure that they know what each card says. Give students suitable dictionaries and ask them to look up a definition for each of the words containing the broad /ô/ sound. After reading the definition for the word, encourage students to write down the word with their own definition.

As an extra challenge for more-confident learners, ask them to put the words into alphabetical order before they write the definitions.

Wrap-Up

Return to the Notebook file and complete the word search on page 4. Ask students to look for words containing the broad /ô/ sound in the word search. Explain that there are six words altogether. Tell students to write the words they find on their individual whiteboards, copying the spelling of the word carefully. Once they have done this, invite volunteers to come to the SMART Board, highlight the words, and write them into the boxes provided on the page. The correct answers can be checked by pressing the red arrow at the top of the screen.

Words Ending in -le

Learning objective
- To spell words using known conventions.

Resources
- "Words Ending in -le" Notebook file
- individual whiteboards and pens

Whiteboard tools
- Eraser
- Pen tray
- Select tool
- Transparency tool
- Highlighter pen

Getting Started

Display the list of words on page 2 of the "Words Ending in -le" Notebook file. Ask students what the words have in common. When they spot the pattern, select the dark blue panel at the top and increase its transparency to reveal the answer. (Go to Properties, click on Fill Effects, and use the slider to adjust the transparency.) Explain that -le is a common spelling pattern in English.

Ask: *Can you think of other words that end in* -le? Add examples to the board and highlight the -le endings.

Mini-Lesson

1. Consider the words on the SMART Board. Does -le always have the same sound? Mention words such as *mile* and *whole*, where -le is not a separate syllable and has no sound of its own.

2. Move on to page 3 of the Notebook file. Tell students that you are holding a spelling bee, setting familiar words for students to say or write on their individual whiteboards. Press the red buttons to hear the words. Invite students to spell the words, then use the Eraser to reveal the correct answers.

3. View the correct spelling of the words that don't end in -le. Point out that their final letters produce the same sound as -le. Ask: *How can you know which letters to use?* Share ideas.

4. Suggest some pointers to help students with spelling. Page 4 offers a useful classroom poster with three such spelling conventions, which can be discussed, highlighted, and added to.

5. Go to page 5. Explain that answers to this crossword are all -le words. Allow thinking time before filling in an agreed answer. If necessary, prompt students with further clues. For example, *4 across is a speech __?* Use the Eraser to reveal the letters in the crossword.

6. Display the chart on page 6, which contains headings representing the main -le family groups: -able, -ckle, *double letter* + le, -dle, -cle, -ble, -ible, -ple. Ask children to help you sort and drag the words to the correct columns.

Independent Work

Ask students to copy the -le chart into their notebooks. Challenge them to add new words to these family groups, perhaps searching for them in their independent reading books. Suggest a minimum of six words per family. Support less-confident learners by directing them toward suitable resources for finding words. Extend the activity by inviting students to highlight words that are new to them and to find out their meanings.

Wrap-Up

Compare results. Use the SMART Board to create a class -le chart, which can be saved for future use. Review any common difficulties with spelling individual words with reference to the chart where necessary. Use this as a starting point for creating a "Difficult -le Words" list on page 7 of the Notebook file to return to in later lessons.

Prefixes *un-* and *dis-*

Learning objective

- To spell with increasing accuracy and confidence, drawing on word recognition and knowledge of word structure.

Resources

- "Prefixes *un-* and *dis-*" Notebook file
- "Add a Prefix" (p. 59), cut apart
- individual whiteboards and pens
- pencils
- paper

Whiteboard tools

- Pen tray
- Select tool

Getting Started

Open page 2 of the "Prefixes *un-* and *dis-*" Notebook file. Ask students to think of words that mean the opposite of *happy*. List all of their ideas, but make sure that *unhappy* is in the list. Repeat this for the words *kind*, *honest*, and *agree*, again ensuring that *unkind*, *dishonest*, and *disagree* are in their respective lists.

Using these lists, first point out *unhappy* and *unkind*, then *dishonest* and *disagree*. Ask students if they notice anything in particular about these words. Elicit that *un-* or *dis-* have been added to the beginnings of these words to change them into words of the opposite meaning.

Mini-Lesson

1. Tell students that *un-* and *dis-* are both prefixes that can be added to the beginning of words to create new words. Explain that these particular prefixes create a new word that means the opposite (or negative) of the original word.

2. With the class, read the words at the bottom of page 3 of the Notebook file. Check that all students understand the meaning of the words. Put the words into context in a sentence, if necessary.

3. Ask students to talk with a partner to decide which prefix should be added to which word to create its opposite.

4. Invite individuals to come to the SMART Board and drag the words into the correct boxes to check the answers. When the words are dragged into the boxes, the prefixes will magically appear.

5. Point out that although *un-* and *dis-* can both be added to *like* and *able*, the two different prefixes give the words two different meanings. Ensure that students understand that they must choose the correct prefix for the context of the sentence.

Independent Work

Give each group a set of "Add a Prefix" cards (p. 59). Ask students to add an appropriate prefix (*un-* or *dis-*) to the words to create new words with opposite meanings. Invite students to write sentences containing the new words. Encourage students to self-check their work with the rest of their group. Invite them to discuss any words on which they have a difference of opinion.

Wrap-Up

Show students page 4 of the Notebook file. Read the sentences with them. Explain that the underlined words need to have a prefix added to them in order to give the sentence the opposite meaning. Give students an opportunity to write down their ideas for each sentence on their individual whiteboards. Once they have done this, invite volunteers to come to the SMART Board and drag a prefix into the appropriate space. Discuss any errors and misconceptions together. Then pull the tab on the left-hand side across the screen to reveal the answers.

Suffixes *-ful* and *-ly*

Learning objective

- To spell words with the common suffixes *-ful* and *-ly*.

Resources

- "Suffixes *-ful* and *-ly*" Notebook file
- "Useful Suffixes" (p. 60)
- individual whiteboards and pens

Whiteboard tools

- Pen tray
- Select tool
- On-screen Keyboard
- Highlighter pen

Getting Started

Orally assign a word to each student that contains either the suffix *-ful* or *-ly*. Ask students to consider how to spell their assigned word, then sort themselves into three groups: *-ful*, *-ly*, and unsure. Together, help the unsure group decide. If required, use page 2 of the "Suffixes *-ful* and *-ly*" Notebook file to write the words to show students how to spell them.

Mini-Lesson

1. Explain that *-ful* and *-ly* are both suffixes that can be added to the end of words to create new words.

2. Read the words at the bottom of page 3 of the Notebook file with students. Check that they all understand the meaning of the words. Put the words into context in a sentence, if necessary.

3. Ask students to talk with a partner to decide which suffix (*-ful* or *-ly*) should be added to each word to create a new word. Then invite volunteers to come to the SMART Board to drag the words into the appropriate box to check the answers.

4. Check whether students understand that the function of the word changes when a suffix is added. Ask them to make sentences on their individual whiteboards incorporating some of the new words. Ask volunteers to write their sentences on page 4 of the Notebook file.

5. Read the sentences on page 5. Ask students to decide which word, from those at the bottom of the page, best fits into each blank.

6. Point to a word at the bottom of the page and ask: *In which sentence does this word belong?* Drag the correct word into each sentence.

7. Point out that when a word ends in *-y*, such as *happy* or *beauty*, the y changes to an *i* before the suffix is added (*happily, beautiful*).

Independent Work

Give each student a copy of "Useful Suffixes" (p. 60). Ask them to fill in the missing word in each sentence, from the selection given. Remind students to check that their sentences make sense.

Adapt the activity for more-confident learners. Simply provide the stems of the words in the word bank (such as *happy* instead of *happily*). They will then need to add the suffix before filling in the missing word. As an extension, ask students to think of more words containing the *-ful* and *-ly* suffix.

Wrap-Up

Share the answers from the independent work as a class and discuss any differences of choice. Go to page 6 of the Notebook file and look at the word search together. Challenge students to locate the six hidden words in less than three minutes. Invite individuals to highlight a word in the grid, then write that word on the lines by the side of the grid. Finally, pull the tab across the screen to reveal the answers.

Antonyms

Learning objective
- To understand that antonyms are words that have the opposite meaning.

Resources
- "Antonyms" Notebook file
- "Antonym Dominoes" (p. 61), copied onto cardstock and cut along the dotted lines into a set of 24 dominoes
- individual whiteboards and pens

Whiteboard tools
- Eraser
- Pen tray
- Delete button
- Select tool

Getting Started

Open the "Antonyms" Notebook file and go to page 2. Show students the picture of the character and work together to make a list of words to describe him. Now ask them to imagine a character that is the opposite of the one on the board and make a list of words to describe this new character.

Mini-Lesson

1. Go to page 3 of the Notebook file and introduce the word *antonym* as a term for a word with an opposite meaning.

2. Read the word at the top of page 4 together and ask students to decide, in pairs, which rocket has the antonym on it.

3. Allow a student to press on the rocket to see if his or her choice is correct. An explosion will be heard if the correct answer is chosen. Alternatively, use the Eraser on the star to reveal whether the answer is correct.

4. Repeat this activity on pages 5 to 7, defining any vocabulary as necessary.

5. Provide each student with an individual whiteboard. Show page 8 and challenge students to write down on their boards, in one minute, as many antonyms as they can for the displayed word.

6. Once they have done this, invite a volunteer to come to the SMART Board and use the Delete button to remove the shape to reveal one antonym. Then let students share any other words they have thought of and add them to the Notebook page.

7. Again, address any errors or misconceptions in students' vocabulary.

8. Repeat this activity on pages 9 to 11.

Independent Work

Divide the class into groups of three students. Give a set of "Antonym Dominoes" (p. 61) to each group and ask them to share out the dominoes equally. Explain that this domino game is exactly the same as normal dominoes, except that students need to match antonyms together instead of numbers or pictures. Encourage students to challenge the antonym choices of other players if they disagree with them.

Allow less-confident learners to play the game in teams of two so that they can support each other in the decision-making process. Challenge more-confident learners to create their own antonym domino game once they have played the version supplied.

Wrap-Up

Go to page 12 of the Notebook file and ask students to explain what an antonym is. Suggest that they explain this to a friend and then share answers as a class. Delete the top yellow shape to reveal a congratulatory message to students. Next, delete the lower yellow shape. Invite students to think of an antonym for *fast*. Repeat for several other words to assess which students have grasped the concept.

Synonyms

Learning objective

- To explore how particular words are used, including words and expressions with similar meanings.

Resources

- "Synonyms" Notebook file
- prepared cards with three different words on each one (choose words that have a few different synonyms, such as *small*, *walk*, and *nice*)
- a thesaurus
- strips of paper
- pencils
- individual whiteboards and pens

Whiteboard tools

- Eraser
- Pen tray
- Select tool
- Undo button
- Delete button

Getting Started

Go to page 2 of the "Synonyms" Notebook file. Look at the picture of the character (Ben). Say two sentences that are the same, except for one word—for example: *Ben is kind. Ben is considerate.* Write these next to Ben.

Ask students to consider the two sentences and decide whether they have the same or a different meaning. Ask students to vote, then look up the definition of both words in a dictionary. Ask: *Do they have the same or a different meaning?* Use the Undo button to reset the page, then repeat the activity a few times, using different describing words.

Mini-Lesson

1. Go to page 3 of the Notebook file and introduce the word *synonym* as a term for words with the same or similar meaning.

2. Read the word at the top of page 4 together. Ask students to decide, in pairs, which balloon has the synonym on it.

3. Allow a student to press on the balloon. If his or her choice is correct, a cheer will be heard. Alternatively, use the Eraser to rub over the balloon to reveal the answer.

4. Repeat this activity on pages 5 to 8, defining any vocabulary as necessary.

5. Provide each student with an individual whiteboard. Display page 9 and challenge students to write down as many synonyms for the word displayed as they can think of in one minute.

6. Choose individuals to write synonyms for the word in the text boxes next to the balloon. Again, address any errors or misconceptions in students' vocabulary.

7. Repeat this activity on pages 10 to 12 of the Notebook file.

8. Introduce students to a simple thesaurus if they have not used one before.

Independent Work

Give each student his or her own prepared card (see Resources). Check that students are able to read the words and understand their meaning. Give each student three strips of paper and ask him or her to write one of the words on the left-hand side of each strip. Encourage students to write as many synonyms for each word as they can think of on its strip. When finished, have students combine all of their completed strips, put them into alphabetical order, and stick them onto a sheet of construction paper or into a scrapbook to form a class thesaurus. Encourage students to add initial letter headings for ease of reference.

Wrap-Up

Go to page 13 of the Notebook file. In pairs, ask students to discuss and explain what a synonym is. Share answers as a class. Use the Delete button to delete the top yellow shape, revealing a congratulatory message to students. Next, delete the lower yellow shape. Challenge students to think of a synonym for *sad*. Repeat this for several other words until you are sure they fully understand the concept.

Homonyms

Learning objective

- To understand that homonyms are words with the same spelling but different meanings.

Resources

- "Homonyms" Notebook file
- writing materials

Whiteboard tools

- Eraser
- Pen tray
- Highlighter pen
- Area Capture tool
- Select tool
- Gallery

Getting Started

Display the sentences on page 2 of the "Homonyms" Notebook file. Allow students a few minutes to study these sentence pairs. What do they notice? (Each pair shares a word.) Highlight these words. What is strange about these words? (They change meaning.) Use the Eraser to reveal that they are called *homonyms*. Ask for synonyms (words of the same meaning) for some of them. Write them at the end of each sentence.

Pull out and discuss the term *homonym*: words that have the same spelling, but different meaning or origin. Identify the Getting Started words as examples. Can students think of other everyday examples? (*Dear*, *light*, *table*, and so on.)

Mini-Lesson

1. Explain that some homonyms have a different sound and a different meaning.

2. Investigate the homonyms on page 2 of the Notebook file. Differentiate homonyms with the same pronunciation (*fit*; *rose*) from those that change pronunciation (*wound*; *bow*). Use two highlighter colors to group the homonyms.

3. Go to page 3 and open the "Homonym Impostors" activity. Explain the game: all except one word are homonyms in each group. After thinking time, invite a student or small group to choose the homonym impostor.

4. You can use the Area Capture tool to take a snapshot of the final pages that list the words that are and are not homonyms.

Independent Work

Use the homonyms listed from the game (shown on page 4 of the Notebook file). Ask students to write a pair of sentences for each homonym. Each pair of sentences must use the homonym with two different meanings.

Support less-confident learners by suggesting that they work with a partner. Alternatively, use illustrations to show different meanings and then write sentences. As an extra challenge, ask students to think of synonyms for the words and invite them to plan a humorous wordplay poem or joke using homonyms.

Wrap-Up

Share answers. Invite students to write their sentences on page 5 of the Notebook file. Supply some appropriate illustrations from the Gallery to highlight the differences. To extend the lesson, or for homework, introduce work on the draft of a class poem using the homonyms and guidance on page 6.

Compound Words

Learning objective

- To spell unfamiliar words using known conventions, including morphological rules.

Resources

- "Compound Words" Notebook file
- individual whiteboards and pens
- printout of the activity on page 6 of the Notebook file, one copy for each pair (optional)

Whiteboard tools

- Eraser
- Pen tray
- Select tool
- On-screen Keyboard
- Delete button

Getting Started

On page 2 of the "Compound Words" Notebook file, show these words: *drawbridge*, *broomstick*, and *earthquake*. What do the words have in common? Use the Eraser to reveal that they are *compound words*. Pull out the definition at the bottom of the page: Compound words occur when words are joined to form a new word. Separate the words on the board to show how and where each one is joined.

Mini-Lesson

1. Explain that the meanings of the different parts of a compound word add together to form the meaning of the new word. Pages 3 to 5 of the Notebook file provide a visual explanation with the word *lifeguard*. Press the hyperlinked arrow to reveal each stage, demonstrating that *life + guard = someone who guards life*.

2. Demonstrate how the three compound words from Getting Started can be broken down in the same way. Separate them and write an addition sign between each pair of words.

3. Explain the activity on page 6: The compound words must be assembled and matched to the correct definitions. Press the image to start the activity.

4. Work on one definition at a time. Invite students to drag and drop the words to create the appropriate compound words. Press the *Am I correct?* button to see if the words have been placed correctly.

5. Move on to page 7. Ask students to look around the room to spot some compound words. Delete the boxes to reveal some possible examples: *classroom*, *whiteboard*, *blackboard*, *cupboard*. Add other compound words that students identify.

6. Separate the compound words. Point out that the word *board* is used in more than one of the compound words.

7. Link your investigations to text-level work on character descriptions. Read a piece of narrative with interesting details about a fictional character. Make sure that the text contains some compound words.

8. Ask students to write, on individual whiteboards, the compound words they hear. Compare and write the results on the SMART Board. Demonstrate how the words can be split in two by addition signs.

Independent Work

Explain that some words appear frequently in compound words. Provide ten base words for students to work with (for the beginning or end of the compound words): *day, no, any, some, time, every, eye, sand, out, play*. For each word, challenge students to find at least two or three compound words that contain the word.

Support less-confident learners by using pictures, with arrows pointing to relevant objects. Challenge students to investigate two pages of a class text, searching for further examples. Add the words to a "Compound Words" bank (see Wrap-Up).

Wrap-Up

Share and display results on page 8 of the Notebook file. Save the page to add compound words in later sessions, and encourage students to keep collecting words.

Words Within Words

Learning objective
- To spell unfamiliar words using known conventions, including morphological rules.

Resources
- "Words Within Words" Notebook file
- "Find the Words" (p. 62)
- individual whiteboards and pens

Whiteboard tools
- Pen tray
- Select tool
- Highlighter pen
- Fill Color tool
- Pen tool

Getting Started
Show page 2 of the "Words Within Words" Notebook file. Explain that the words shown have something in common. Can students identify what it is? Provide more clues if necessary to help students to recognize that all the words contain the word *in*. Highlight this in each example. Pull the tab to reveal the answer.

Mini-Lesson
1. Explain that many words in English have other words within them. A word within a word must have all its letters next to one another and in the correct order.

2. Show students the different names on pages 3 to 6 of the Notebook file. Ask them to think about each name in turn and to write (and then hold up) one inside word for each name on their individual whiteboards. Once everyone is agreed, double-click on the name, highlight those letters, and drag the inside word to the space provided.

3. Repeat until students cannot find any more inside words. Finally, press the green box and use the Fill Color tool to fill it with white and reveal the words. Repeat for pages 4 to 6.

4. Give students time to investigate their own names. Compare results.

5. If there is time, try the words on page 7. Let students come to the SMART Board to write their words. Ask the other students: *Are the letters next to one another? Are they in the correct order?*

6. After a student has recorded a word within a word, give someone else the chance to identify and record a different word. (Convert handwritten words to text by selecting them and selecting the Recognize option from the drop-down menu.)

7. Check the answers by pressing on the red box.

Independent Work
Distribute a copy of "Find the Words" (p. 62) to each student. Ask students to list the words they can find. Remind them that the letters must be next to each other. Encourage them to use a dictionary when needed.

Support less-confident learners by providing some initial letters. Challenge students to create a new vocabulary list linked to math or science. Each word on the list must contain at least two other words within it.

Wrap-Up
Share the results using page 9 of the Notebook file. Check that a word's letters are all in the correct order on the SMART Board. Make use of the Highlighter pen to identify unusual answers. Regularly point out that remembering the hidden words helps with remembering the spelling of the longer word. Press the red box to reveal the answers.

Alphabetical Order

Learning objective
- To put text in alphabetical order.

Resources
- "Alphabetical Order" Notebook file
- Internet access
- Web site containing lists of books such as *www.scholastic. com*
- individual whiteboards and pens
- a dictionary or thesaurus for each group

(Microsoft Word is required to view the embedded text document in the Notebook file.)

Whiteboard tools
- Pen tray
- Select tool
- On-screen Keyboard
- Area Capture tool

Getting Started

Divide the class into groups of three. Give each group a thesaurus. Display page 2 of the "Alphabetical Order" Notebook file and assign one adjective to each group. Allow two minutes for the group to find a synonym for it. Open the text document, which presents the synonyms in a table format. Collect and type the results. For example: *humorous = funny*; *contented = happy*; and so on. Use Microsoft Word's Thesaurus to check the validity of each synonym.

Ask students: *Are these words in any particular order? Can you think of a way to make it easy to find a word in this list?*

Mini-Lesson

1. Use your computer's Web browser to view a bookstore Web site, such as *www.scholastic.com* (press the link to the Scholastic Teachers' Store). Ask students for suggestions as to how you would search for a particular title. You could, for example, browse the store by subject or by grade level. Lead them to see that books can be listed in alphabetical order. Discuss the benefits of using alphabetical order.

2. Exit the Internet and return to the Notebook file. On page 3, prompt students to think of some uses for alphabetical order in classroom organization. Press the button in the lower right of the page for some suggestions.

3. Open the "Alphabetical Texts" activity on page 4. Explain the scenario: the library books are not in order. How can the librarians help themselves and their users? (Use alphabetical order.)

4. With students' help, drag and drop the books onto the shelves in alphabetical order. Encourage students to use the on-screen alphabet as a guide.

5. Discuss difficulties—for example, two books may begin with the same word so later words need to be considered. Finally, press the *Am I correct?* button to see if the books are correctly placed.

6. If you would like to keep the correct sequence for reference, use the Area Capture tool to take a snapshot, which you can add to the current Notebook page.

7. Explain that you have some new (short) titles to add. Call out a title at a time and ask students to write, on individual whiteboards, which book it should follow. Check and discuss the answers.

Independent Work

Ask students to look around the classroom and write a list (in alphabetical order) for a classroom guide to important resources.

Support less-confident learners by suggesting items for the list. As an extra challenge, ask students to provide a further section of the classroom guide (such as a code of conduct) in alphabetical order.

Wrap-Up

Scan or type students' lists onto page 5. (Upload scanned lists by selecting Insert, then Picture File, and browsing to where you have saved them.) Point out places where alphabetical order was tricky (perhaps two words beginning with the same letter).

Firework Poem

Learning objective

- To make adventurous word and language choices appropriate to the style and purpose of the text.

Resources

- "Firework Poem" Notebook file
- fireworks video (search video Websites, such as youtube.com)
- paper
- pencils
- black paper
- chalk or oil pastels

Whiteboard tools

- Pen tray
- Select tool
- On-screen Keyboard
- Lines tool
- Shapes tool

Getting Started

With the class, watch a video of some fireworks. Ask students to observe the different sights and sounds. Suggest that they think of interesting words to describe what they can see (such as *whoosh* and *twinkle*). After they have finished watching the video, invite them to talk with a partner about what they saw and heard. Suggest that they could also describe to each other any firework displays that they have seen.

Mini-Lesson

1. Open the "Firework Poem" Notebook file. Show students the shape poem on page 2. Ask them to describe what they can see. If necessary, point out the shape of the Catherine wheel and the launching and exploding rocket.

2. Read the poem with students, encouraging them to add expression. For example, shout the word *bang* and hiss the word *fizz*.

3. Move back and forth between pages 2, 3, and 4 to see the poem change to give the effect of fireworks.

4. Comment on the type of words used in the poem and how they were used. Ensure that students realize that the words describe either the sound or appearance of a firework.

5. Go to page 5 of the Notebook file. Ask students to read the words at the bottom of the page. Invite them to sort the words into two boxes: words that describe the sound and words that describe the appearance of the fireworks. Clarify the meaning of any words that students are unsure about.

6. Use page 6 to create a class firework poem. Suggest to students that they could use the words from page 5 and remind them of the shapes and sounds from the video.

7. Support students in rotating, resizing, and altering the color of the text as necessary. Show them how to use the Shapes and Lines tools to illustrate their class poem if they wish to do so.

Independent Work

Tell students that they are going to produce a firework shape poem. Encourage them to make a list of possible words on some scrap paper. Give each student a sheet of black paper and some chalk or oil pastels to create the final poem (make the pastel tips as sharp as possible). Suggest that students use a pencil first to draw a faint outline of the firework shapes that their words are going to follow.

Wrap-Up

Take a small sample of students' work and scan it into the computer. Display the work using the SMART Notebook software; selected examples can be added to page 7 of the Notebook file. (Upload digital pictures of students' work by selecting Insert, then Picture File, and browsing to where you have saved the images.) Invite the class to comment on the poems. Write some of these comments around the pictures. Evaluate the shapes and vocabulary used within the poems. Encourage positive comments from students.

Organizing Ideas

earning objective
▸ To explain organizational features of texts, including layout, diagrams, and captions.

Resources
"Organizing Ideas" Notebook file
"Making a Pizza" (p. 63)
building blocks
scissors
paper
felt-tipped pens

Whiteboard tools
Pen tray
Select tool

Getting Started

Display page 2 of the "Organizing Ideas" Notebook file. Have students work in pairs. Using building blocks, ask one student in each pair to create a simple model using only five pieces—without showing their partner. Ask these students to give verbal instructions to their partner so that they can make a replica of the model.

Invite students to assess how easy or difficult they found this task. Ask: *Can you think of anything that would have made it easier?* Encourage suggestions (e.g. it may have been easier with visual instructions). Write these suggestions on the Notebook page.

Mini-Lesson

1. Look at the pictures on page 3 of the Notebook file. Talk about the pictures with students.

2. Explain that the pictures could be used to create a set of instructions for how to make a clay model. Ask students to consider how to present these instructions.

3. Encourage them to use the arrows to show the order of the instructions. Let them add numbers if they suggest this.

4. Repeat the process on page 4, but this time, emphasize the importance of putting the pictures in the correct order.

5. Show students that it is not possible to fit all of the pictures in a line across the page. Point out that if you put the pictures on two or three lines they may be difficult to follow. Ask students to suggest what to do so that the instructions are still easy to follow. Did they choose to order and display the pictures in a different way from the previous page?

6. Ask students to evaluate, with a partner, whether the instructions are organized in a useful and easy-to-follow way. Ask them to suggest any improvements.

Independent Work

Give each student a copy of "Making a Pizza" (p. 63). Ask them to cut out and then order the instructions. Supply paper and felt-tipped pens. Ask students to consider how to organize the instructions to show clearly how the pizza should be made. Remind them that they could use arrows, numbers, and boxes.

Challenge more-confident learners to write their own instructions, as well as organize these clearly on the page.

Wrap-Up

Discuss some of the work created and evaluate whether it is clear to follow. Show students page 5 of the Notebook file and ask them to read each of the instructions. Invite them to work in pairs to decide the order in which the instructions should be followed. Ask: *How can we show this clearly?* Invite individuals to move the instructions on the screen so that they can be clearly followed. Students could vote to decide on the correct place in the order for each instruction.

Following Directions

Learning objective

- To explain organizational features of texts, including layout, diagrams, captions, and bullet points.

Resources

- "Following Directions" Notebook file
- "How to Make a Stick Puppet" (p. 64)
- bread
- butter
- cheese
- plate
- plastic knife
- white card
- tape
- straws
- felt-tipped pens
- scissors
- pencils

Whiteboard tools

- Pen tray
- Select tool
- Highlighter pen

Getting Started

Open the "Following Directions" Notebook file and display page 2. Ask: *What are directions?* Give students simple directions and let them carry them out. For example: *Put your left hand on your head.* Point out that giving directions is like giving an order, and it makes you sound bossy!

Ask students to tell a partner who might need to give directions, and why. Talk about giving directions—consider how a teacher gives directions to tell students what work to do and how students might give directions to teach a friend a new game, and so on. Make notes on page 2, if required.

Mini-Lesson

1. Read the directions on page 3 of the Notebook file. Discuss how the directions are presented: for example, they are numbered, written in the order they are to be carried out.

2. Ask students to identify the bossy words (verbs) in the directions and invite individuals to come to the SMART Board and highlight them on the page.

3. Read each direction again, one at a time, and allow a student to carry out each of the steps to make the sandwich.

4. When the sandwich is made, evaluate the finished product. Ask: *Were the directions detailed enough? Did the sandwich turn out the way you expected it to?*

5. Show students page 4. Give them the opportunity to read each direction.

6. Challenge them to work out the order in which the directions should be. Invite students to come to the board to rearrange them so that they are correct.

7. Once they have done this, read the directions together to check that they are ordered correctly.

Independent Work

Give each student a copy of "How to Make a Stick Puppet" (p. 64). Ask them to read it carefully to themselves. Put white card, tape, straws, scissors, pencils, and felt-tipped pens on each table. Challenge students to follow the directions on their sheet to create a stick puppet. Point out key structural features of the directions as you work with students (such as bossy words, numbered points, and so on).

Support less-confident learners with reading any tricky words while encouraging them to have a go at reading key words independently. Set a challenge for more-confident learners by rearranging the directions and asking them to put these into the correct order before they begin to follow them.

Wrap-Up

Ask students to explain what a direction sentence needs. Show students page 5 of the Notebook file and ask them to read each statement. Challenge them to identify which of the statements are directions. Allow them to highlight the statements they believe are directions. The sentences can then be sorted into two groups. Discuss students' choices together as a class.

Retelling an Event

earning objectives

To write simple and compound sentences and begin to use subordination in relation to time and reason.
To compose sentences using tense consistently (present and past).

esources

"Retelling an Event"
Notebook file
paper
pencils

Vhiteboard tools

Pen tray
Highlighter pen
Select tool
On-screen
Keyboard

Getting Started

Open the "Retelling an Event" Notebook file and read page 2 together. Introduce the text as a retelling of an event, explaining that retelling gives a chronological account of an event that has taken place. Point out a transition word in the text (such as *next* or *then*) and explain that a transition word is a linking word that can be used to give more information about the time that something happened. Together, identify other transition words in the text and highlight them.

Mini-Lesson

1. Ask students to describe to a partner how they get ready for school—from waking up to leaving the house.

2. Display the pictures on page 3 of the Notebook file. Ask students to describe what is happening in each picture.

3. Explain to students that they are going to write a retelling of how the boy in the picture (Charlie) got ready for school this morning.

4. Discuss how a retelling is usually written in chronological order, then allow students time to order the pictures correctly on the board. Talk about the words at the bottom of the page, explaining that they will help in writing the retelling.

5. Work as a class to write a retelling of how Charlie got ready for school this morning, using page 4 of the Notebook file.

6. Take suggestions from students and model good retelling. Emphasize that a retelling is usually written in the past tense, in chronological order, and includes transition words.

7. Read back the finished piece and evaluate whether these criteria have been met.

Independent Work

Ask students to write a retelling of a simple, recent event, such as planting a seed. Suggest that they start by drawing up a simple list of five main events that they are going to include in their piece. Refer students back to the transition words discovered in Getting Started and challenge them to use at least five transition words in their recount.

Give less-confident learners pictures of the main events that they need to include and a list of transition words to support their writing.

Wrap-Up

Give students time to check their work and ask them to use a colored pencil to underline any transition words they have used. Ask them to check that they have included their target of five transition words in their work. Invite some of students to read aloud their pieces. Ask the rest of the class to raise their hands every time they hear a transition word being used. List these on page 5 of the Notebook file. Use this opportunity to assess students' understanding of transition words. Page 6 offers further opportunities to understand transition words.

Time Signals

Learning objectives
- To signal sequence, place, and time to give coherence.
- To show relation-ships of time, reason, and cause through subordination and transitions.

Resources
- "Time Signals" Notebook file
- individual white-boards and pens

Whiteboard tools
- Pen tray
- Highlighter pen
- On-screen Keyboard
- Blank Page button

Getting Started

Play "All Change!" Set an event for students to retell to a partner. After one minute, call "All change!" where speakers and listeners swap roles. At the next "All change!" announce a new topic. Listen to conversations, sometimes providing contributions. Finish with a retelling of your morning, overusing *and then* and *then*. For example:

I came into the building. Then I went to the staffroom for a coffee and then I came to the classroom. I put up a poster and then I put some writing around it. Then I marked the math books and then the writing books. Then I did some work on the computer and then I went to fetch my class.

Ask students to offer any criticism they have of the words you used.

Mini-Lesson

1. Did students notice your repetitions? Write the repeated words on a new Notebook page. Discuss the use of those words: to make incidents follow on from one another in a time sequence.

2. Discuss how retelling needs chronological sequences. Ask students to think about their earlier retelling. Did they or their partner link parts of an event in sequence? Did they overuse any words?

3. Repeat your story from the Getting Started activity, this time using a variety of words and phrases to signal time sequence. Ask students to jot down on individual whiteboards the time words they identify. Share results, listing words and phrases on the SMART Board.

4. Go to page 2 of the "Time Signals" Notebook file. Point out that this is a narrative text, but that the time sequence helps the audience's understanding. Work with students, identifying words and phrases that signal time sequences.

5. Give thinking time, directing students to search in a particular paragraph. Highlight the answers: *now, after, next, meanwhile*.

6. On a new Notebook page, write the following phrases: *later, afterward, eventually, suddenly, just, immediately, at once, from now on*. Point out that these phrases can also be used to show time when telling a story. Discuss what each phrase means.

7. Choose a recent school event and discuss important incidents within the event. Not six to eight incidents on a new page of the SMART Board, but not in time order.

Independent Work

Ask students to write a retelling (in the past tense) of the event, using a variety of words and phrases to signal time sequence. Link this to other text work, such as a letter to a friend or relation. Support less-confident learners by ordering the incidents.

Wrap-Up

As students read their recounts, ask listeners to identify any words that signal time sequences. Play a final game of "All Change!" with students monitoring each other's language. Has their use of time words improved?

Story Setting

Learning objectives

To explain ideas and processes using imaginative and adventurous vocabulary.
To make adventurous word and language choices appropriate to the style and purpose of the text.

Resources

"Story Setting" Notebook file
"Story Settings" (p. 65) with the cards cut apart
individual whiteboards and pens
paint
chalk
felt-tipped pens
paper and card
picture book with clear illustrations of settings

Whiteboard tools

Pen tray
Spotlight tool
Select tool
Screen Shade

Getting Started

Look at a picture book with clear illustrations that show the setting of the story. Ask students to think about where the story is set and listen to their ideas. Focus on one of the illustrations and invite students to describe the setting to a partner. Challenge them to use interesting descriptive vocabulary to do this.

Make notes on page 2 of the "Story Settings" Notebook file. Share some of students' ideas as a whole class.

Mini-Lesson

1. Go to page 3 of the Notebook file and look in detail at the pictures of the three settings.

2. Focus on one setting at a time using the Spotlight tool or the Screen Shade.

3. Ask students to choose the setting that they are most interested in and describe it to a partner. Share some of these descriptions as a class on page 4.

4. Give students individual whiteboards and ask them to list five words or phrases that could be used when writing a description of their chosen setting. Share some of these ideas as a class.

5. Using pages 5 to 7, ask students to match the setting descriptions to the illustrations and to explain why they think they have chosen the correct one. Discuss any vocabulary that is unfamiliar to them.

Independent Work

Give each group a set of four cards prepared from "Story Settings" (p. 65). Ask students to choose a card and read the story setting description on it. Talk about the type of setting that their card describes. Provide students with materials such as paint, chalk, or felt-tipped pens to create a piece of artwork that illustrates the setting description on their card. Encourage students to talk to one another about their setting and discuss ideas about how to illustrate the setting.

Wrap-Up

Take a few samples of students' artwork and scan them into the computer. (Upload scanned images of students' work by selecting Insert, then Picture File, and browsing to where you have saved the images.) Display the work on page 8 of the Notebook file and ask the class to comment on it. Write some of their comments around the picture. Ask: *Which setting description do you think this is illustrating?* Evaluate whether the work includes all of the details that were given in the description. Compare different illustrations of the same description. Comment how a more detailed description should give a more accurate picture.

Setting and Atmosphere

Learning objective
- To select and use descriptive vocabulary.

Resources
- "Setting and Atmosphere" Notebook file
- individual whiteboards and pens
- paper and pens

Whiteboard tools
- Pen tray
- Select tool
- Spotlight tool
- Highlighter pen
- On-screen Keyboard

Getting Started
Talk to students about the familiar places in which stories are often set, such as a school, a home, or a town. Point out that the places are often ordinary. Ask: *How does the writer give them a special atmosphere?* Share views, emphasizing the importance of the author's choice of words. Show page 2 of the "Setting and Atmosphere" Notebook file and ask students for some words to describe the elements in the picture.

Mini-Lesson
1. Explain that the photograph on page 3 of the Notebook file shows a setting for a story. Question students about the picture. For example: *What is shown in the photograph? Who is in the picture? What are they doing?*

2. Use the Spotlight tool to focus on aspects of the photograph and ask: *What word describes this setting? How does the setting make you feel? What time of year is it?* (Adjust the transparency of the Spotlight tool to 50% through the drop-down menu.

3. Pull out the different descriptive words hidden in the picture (by pulling the tabs at the side of the picture).

4. Agree on a collection of descriptive words that describe the scene, taking into account different viewpoints. For example, some people find shopping interesting, while others think that it is boring. Write about 12 descriptive words in the box next to the picture. Copy and paste these words onto page 4 (select the words, select Copy from the drop-down menu, then Paste onto the next page).

5. Explain that you are going to write the opening description to a story. You want your reader to form a good mental picture. Demonstrate how to construct up to four sentences about the photograph, using the different parts of the sentence—subject, verb, and ending—and highlight each part in different colors if necessary.

6. Ask students to close their eyes as you read your description aloud. Invite them to form a picture in their minds. Return to the image on page 3 for students to compare it with their mental picture.

7. Now ask students to think about their classroom. It is going to be the setting for a story. First, they must give the reader a vivid picture.

8. Share some descriptive words about objects and students' feelings about the classroom. Write some ideas on page 5 of the Notebook file.

Independent Work
Ask students to jot down additional atmospheric words about the classroom. Invite them to use these words, and some from page 5 of the Notebook file, to write a description of the classroom in four to six sentences. Press the Hints box on page 5 to show suitable words.

Wrap-Up
Invite students to read their descriptions to the class. Challenge the others to identify the descriptive words used. Add any new words to page 5 of the Notebook file. Type some of the descriptions on the board onto page 6 and save them for future lessons.

Character Profiles

Learning objective
- To make adventurous word and language choices appropriate to the style and purpose of the text.

Resources
- "Build Your Own" file
- "Character Profile" (p. 66)
- a set of cards with well-known character names, such as Cinderella, Goldilocks, the Three Little Pigs, and so on

Whiteboard tools
- Pen tray
- Select tool
- Text tool
- Shapes tool
- Lines tool
- Gallery

Before You Start

Open the "Build Your Own" file on the Main Menu page. Use it to prepare a Notebook file with images from the English folder under Year 3 in the My Content folder in the Gallery. Insert pictures of two contrasting fairytale characters and place them side-by-side, typing a selection of descriptive words and phrases for each character at the bottom. On a new page create a template identical to the "Character Profile" reproducible (p. 66). Include a picture of one of the previously chosen characters.

Getting Started

Open the prepared "Build Your Own" file (see Before You Start) and identify the two characters and the stories they come from. Give students one minute to describe the two characters to a partner. Read the descriptive words and phrases at the bottom of the page and ask students to decide which character they think each word or phrase best describes. Drag the words to the character they describe.

Mini-Lesson

1. Show students the "Character Profile" template on the Notebook file. Recap the words and phrases used to describe the character.

2. Discuss how to complete the character profile. Explain that the information does not have to be written in sentences. With students' help, write in the information. Encourage the use of adjectives.

3. When the character profile is complete, read the information on it. Demonstrate how to use this information to write a passage describing the character.

4. Encourage students to suggest how the information on the card could be turned into proper sentences. Write or type some sentences below the card.

5. Evaluate the finished character description for accuracy. Ask: *Would you be able to identify who the character was by listening to this description?*

Independent Work

Give each group a set of the cards displaying a variety of well-known character names (see Resources). Ask each student to choose a card and to create an ID card for their selected character using "Character Profile" (p. 66). Encourage students to use descriptive and thoughtful language. When the ID card is complete, ask students to write a passage to describe the same character. Encourage them to refer back to the key words and phrases that they used on the ID card.

Wrap-Up

Ask some students to read out their profiles while the others listen. Explain that if a profile has been written well, the listeners should be able to identify the character being described. Ask the listeners if they can identify the character—what words or phrases gave them the biggest clue? If students cannot identify the character, ask the reader to state who the character was. Take suggestions from the listeners about what needs to be included in the description to make it more obvious. Scan some of students' ID cards and display them on a Notebook page. Hide the names and see if the rest of the class can guess who the characters are.

Narrative and Dialogue

Learning objective
- To clarify meaning through the use of quotation marks.

Resources
- "Narrative and Dialogue" Notebook file
- "The Mystery Grows" (p. 67)

Whiteboard tools
- Pen tray
- Highlighter pen (customize the Highlighter pen to include new colors)

Getting Started

Improvise a drama. Ask another adult to leave the room and then return looking unwell. Read out the following extract:

It was 11 o'clock in Class 3. The literacy lesson had already started. Mr. Singh suddenly went out of the room. Then he returned looking miserable.

"You must whisper," groaned Mr. Singh when he came back. "My head is aching."

"If you're ill," replied Mrs. Bloggs, looking at him, "you can go home."

"That's very kind of you," said Mr. Singh as he packed his bag. "I'll try to be back tomorrow."

Mrs. Bloggs continued teaching the class.

Ask students to recall what was said. Repeat the scene if necessary and write it on page 2 of the Notebook file. (Use the Recognize option to convert handwriting into typed text.) Compare it to the completed version on page 3.

Mini-Lesson

1. Read the text on page 3 of the Notebook file with students. Count and write on the board the number of paragraphs (five). Point out instances of new paragraphs (when someone speaks; different paragraphs for different speakers).

2. Examine sentences containing narrative and dialogue. Ask students to work in pairs to look for other punctuation conventions. Compare findings. Stress that the first word spoken always starts with a capital letter and that a punctuation mark (often a comma) separates narrative and speech.

3. Write all of these identified features on the right-hand side of page 3. Highlight examples of commas separating speech from narrative.

4. Focus on the second paragraph. Invite a student volunteer to be Mr. Singh and say his words. Highlight his words and explain that they are interrupted by narrative. Highlight the narrative words in a different color.

5. Repeat the process for the next paragraph, identifying *replied Mrs. Bloggs, looking at him* as part of the narrative. (Be consistent in color highlighting.)

6. Draw students' attention to the use of either periods or commas after speech or narrative (depending on whether the sentence is finished or not).

Independent Work

Explain that "The Mystery Grows" (p. 67) is the second chapter in a story. Students must fill in the gaps to complete the chapter.

Support less-confident learners by directing them toward the picture for each blank. Challenge more-confident learners to write Chapter 3, using a similar mixture of speech and narrative.

Wrap-Up

Go to page 4 of the Notebook file and review students' versions of Chapter 2. Add some of their suggestions to the board. Identify narrative and dialogue and highlight the accurate use of quotation marks and punctuation.

Perspective and Character

Learning objective
- To empathize with characters.

Resources
- "Narrative and Dialogue" Notebook file (with page 4 text completed)
- "The Mystery Grows" (p. 67, completed from the "Narrative and Dialogue" lesson)

(A word-processing program, such as Microsoft Word, will be required to edit text on screen.)

Whiteboard tools
- Pen tray
- On-screen Keyboard

Getting Started
Tell students a brief story about your day. Make a point of using *I* as much as possible and include your feelings as well as your behavior in the story. Invite students to ask you questions. Next, invite a student to tell the story of his or her day. Make sure that *I* is used throughout.

Mini-Lesson
1. Copy and paste, into a text document, your saved text about Mr. Singh and Mrs. Bloggs from pages 3 and 4 of the "Narrative and Dialogue" Notebook file.

2. Discuss what happens in the story, perhaps adding new details. Talk about the characters. What is Mr. Singh like? What sort of person is Mrs. Bloggs? What do you think about each character's behavior? Refer to the text to support views.

3. Explain that the story is written in the third person — the characters are seen through the eyes of the author.

4. Highlight a place where Mr. Singh is referred to as *he*. Identify it as a third-person pronoun. Remind students of the first-person pronoun (*I*). Replace the highlighted word with *I*. Use the word-processing program's Find and Replace function to change all of the pronouns to *I*.

5. Read the changed text aloud. Discuss the effect of the new words (confusion). Emphasize that writers must use pronouns consistently, or readers will be unsure whose name a pronoun refers to.

6. Talk about writing a story in the first person. What are the advantages? (A character speaks for himself and the reader may learn more about the character's thoughts.)

7. Model narrative writing in the first person (as Mrs. Bloggs), for example:

   I was explaining pronouns to Class 3 when a noise distracted me. I felt cross because this was an important lesson. I noticed...

8. Highlight these as first-person pronouns. The story has become a first-person narrative account. Is this an interesting and informative way to tell the story?

Independent Work
Ask students to retell this story, writing a first-person account. They must decide which character to be, Mr. Singh or Mrs. Bloggs. Suggest that they do not have to keep to your story; they may add or change incidents. Encourage students to keep checking that they are staying in the first person.

Support less-confident learners by providing some sentences beginning with *I*. As an extra challenge, ask students to choose the other character and write another account in the first person.

Wrap-Up
Ask students to read their narratives to the class. Does the writer stay in the first person? Ask listeners to be alert for slips in pronoun consistency.

Story Planning in Paragraphs

Learning objective
- To group related material into paragraphs.

Resources
- "Build Your Own" file
- "Story Planning in Paragraphs" (p. 68)
- piece of text with at least three paragraphs (type the text on a blank Notebook page)
- individual white-boards and pens
- writing notebooks

Whiteboard tools
- Pen tray
- Gallery
- Select tool
- Highlighter pen
- Shapes tool
- Blank Page button

Before You Start
Prepare a scene on the SMART Board taken from Red Riding Hood using images from the English folder in the "Build Your Own" file (click on the button in the Main Menu, then find it under Year 3 in the My Content folder in the Gallery). Start with the background road scene and add images, resizing as necessary.

Getting Started
Display a piece of text that incorporates at least three paragraphs. Highlight where each paragraph begins. Explain that a paragraph is a group of sentences that fit well together. Discuss the benefits of paragraphs to the reader and writer. Read through the example on the board.

Mini-Lesson
1. Show the prepared picture of Little Red Riding Hood (see Before You Start). Write single words about the setting and characters. Explain that you want to write a shortened version of the story in three planned paragraphs.

2. Move to a blank page and create three rectangles, one under the other. (Use the Shapes tool to make boxes.) Number them 1, 2, and 3. Type a short planning sentence in the first box. For example: *Red Riding Hood went on a journey.*

3. On individual whiteboards, ask students to write short planning sentences for the other two paragraphs (for the next stages in the story).

4. Compare results. Finalize your three planning sentences and type them in the boxes. Stress that this is the plan, not the story. Ask: *What does the plan tell you?* (To write three paragraphs; what to write about in each paragraph.)

5. Choose a title for the story. Model writing paragraph one. Use an opening phrase and write approximately three sentences. Clone the title and the first paragraph and drag to a new page.

6. Assign the first, second, and third sentences of the second paragraph to different pairs of students, having them write their sentence on individual whiteboards.

7. Listen to students' ideas and type in sentences for paragraph two. Clone the paragraph plan and put it in place on the second page of the Notebook file. Emphasize that the new paragraph begins on the next line, its first word indented. Repeat the process for paragraph three.

8. Read the story aloud. Ask questions such as: *Does it sound right? Is a finishing phrase needed? Are there linking words at the start of paragraphs two and three?* After any necessary changes, incorporate additional images from the Gallery and print the page.

Independent Work
Invite students to plan a story for 2nd graders. Give each student a copy of page 68 and invite them to complete the Ideas section and the three planning sentences.

Wrap-Up
Ask some students to demonstrate their planning on the SMART Board. Refer back to the Red Riding Hood story and discuss how helpful it was to plan the story in paragraphs.

Creating a Storyboard

Learning objective
- To signal sequence, place, and time to give coherence.

Resources
- "Creating a Storyboard" Notebook file
- individual whiteboards and pens

Whiteboard tools
- Pen tray
- Select tool
- Area Capture tool
- Fill Color tool

Getting Started

Show page 2 of the "Creating a Storyboard" Notebook file and discuss how you might make a story out of the content. Ask: *How would you continue the story?* Annotate the screen with some of the students' ideas and opinions. Ask students about the type of story likely to result. *What genre is it likely to be?* Go to page 3 and discuss and make a note of the features of a *fable*.

Mini-Lesson

1. Move to page 4 of the Notebook file. Press the image to open "The Hare and the Tortoise" sequencing activity. Ask students to look at the pictures and discuss them with a partner.

2. Discuss what students think is happening in the pictures. Ask: *Which events are important? Is there a main character?* Exchange views.

3. Ask students what is wrong with the pictures. (They are in the wrong order.) Allow students time to think and decide what the picture order should be.

4. Share answers. Question possibilities, debating and experimenting with different orders. Emphasize the need for a correct sequence to be logical.

5. Agree on final selections and drag the pictures into the correct sequence. Are there any surprises? Compare the correct sequence with students' predictions. Were there any points they had not thought about?

6. Point out that a correctly sequenced set of pictures forms a storyboard: it is an effective method of planning a story. Ask: *What genre could the story be?* (A fable)

7. Remind students of your Getting Started text and your discussion on genre. Discuss the essential elements of a fable (see page 5).
   - It is a complete story.
   - Most characters are animals.
   - The animals behave like people.
   - A fable teaches a lesson or a moral.
   - The moral is advice to people about how to live.
   - The moral links with what has happened in the story.

8. Reveal each of the elements as they are correctly identified.

Independent Work

Ask students to use a picture storyboard to plan a fable of their own. Suggest the animals or moral involved if necessary. Stress the importance of the correct sequence for the pictures. Encourage students to ask themselves: *Could someone else follow this plan correctly?*

Wrap-Up

Scan in some completed storyboards and display them on page 6 of the Notebook file. Could other students write a story, with the plot in the correct order, from these story plans? Discuss ideas for one complete story.

Story Planning

Learning objectives

- To use beginning, middle, and end to write narratives in which events are sequenced logically.
- To signal sequence, place, and time to give coherence.

Resources

- "Story Planning" Notebook file
- "Story Planner" (p. 69)

Whiteboard tools

- Pen tray
- Select tool
- Text tool
- On-screen Keyboard
- Spotlight tool

Getting Started

Remind students of the story from "Narrative and Dialogue" (p. 34). Show page 2 of the "Story Planning" Notebook file, which includes a series of incidents from the story, positioned out of sequence. Point out that the story will not work without a plan. Ask students to think about grouping the information into four chapters and adding to it if time is available. Move the notes around the SMART Board until the information is sequenced to students' satisfaction.

Mini-Lesson

1. Move to page 3 of the Notebook file. Explain that this is an author's plan for a mystery story. Pull the tab to reveal details of the first chapter. Talk about the incidents mentioned in the first box. Stress their logical sequence.

2. Move to the Chapter 2 box. Discuss how events are building up. Are students reminded of a familiar story?

3. Invite students to suggest probable ideas for the third chapter. Compare the class's ideas with what is revealed.

4. Discuss what the author must plan to do in the final chapter (resolve the mystery and bring the story to a conclusion). Share some ideas for the author's plan. Compare students' ideas with what is revealed.

5. Ask what students would call the story and each chapter. Use the Eraser to reveal the suggested titles.

6. Discuss the completed plan. Point out that a plan is written before the real story. Do students think they would find it easy to come back to this plan a few days later and write the story?

7. Emphasize the helpful elements of this plan:

   - The shape of the plan (a hill shape reminds the author to build up details before coming down the other side of the hill with the ending)
   - A title
   - Sequence of chapters and chapter headings
   - Notes of incidents to occur in each chapter
   - Clear notes, without too much confusing detail

Independent Work

Ask students to plan their own mystery story using the "Story Planner" (p. 69) with a title, four chapters (with chapter titles), and details for each chapter. Stress the use of clear notes rather than whole sentences. Suggest that students base their mystery story on a familiar story.

Wrap-Up

Scan and display some of the students' plans on page 4 of the Notebook file. Invite individuals to talk about their plans. Suggest that they use the Spotlight tool to bring important points to the class's attention.

Editing Unnecessary Words

Learning objectives

- To make decisions about form and purpose; identify success criteria.
- To compose sentences using adjectives, verbs, and nouns for precision, clarity, and impact.

Resources

- "Editing Unnecessary Words" Notebook file
- "Essential Words" (p. 70)

(Microsoft Word is required to view the embedded text document in the Notebook file.)

Whiteboard tools

- Pen tray
- Select tool
- Highlighter pen
- On-screen Keyboard
- Dual Page

Getting Started

Display page 2 of the "Editing Unnecessary Words" Notebook file. Read the sentence to students: *Quietly and miserably, the unhappy girl with no key shivered in her thin coat in the front garden.*

Suggest that you have been writing a story, but are short of space. Ask students to help you shorten this sentence. Experiment with students' suggestions on the SMART Board. Ask: *Which words are essential? Which words are not so important?* Highlight the important and less-important words in different colors. Stress that the passage must make sense and retain its core meaning.

Mini-Lesson

1. Go to page 3 of the Notebook file. Ask students to read the text and tell you what it is about.

2. Point out that students' oral summaries were quite short. Press the hyperlinked button to open an editable version of the text. Find the word count of the written text (using the Word Count tool in Microsoft Word). Explain that you need to reduce this text to no more than 75 words without losing the sense of the text.

3. Work through the text, sentence by sentence. Ask students to identify and highlight key words in sentences.

4. Repeat the investigation, identifying words that are unnecessary (such as *precious*, *strict*, *sensible*). Highlight these in a different color. Discuss if further reductions could be made. Which words are also unnecessary?

5. Now delete some of the highlighted unnecessary words in the second version of the text. Keep checking that the text makes sense and undo any mistakes. Agree on a final version.

6. Compare the edited text with the original text. (Use Dual Page to view two versions of the "Healthy Teeth" text simultaneously.) Point out how some of the original details were useful (as long as the writer had room for them), but some were unnecessary because they repeated obvious information. Which version of the text do students prefer? Why?

Independent Work

Ask students to complete "Essential Words" (p. 70). They need to rewrite sentences using fewer words.

Support less-confident learners by suggesting they work with a partner, underlining adjectives and unnecessary detail. Check their progress before they start to rewrite the sentences. As an extra challenge, ask students to look at a recent piece of writing. Are there places where shorter sentences would have been better? Can they identify unnecessary words?

Wrap-Up

Compare results. Type the shortest versions on page 4 of the Notebook file. Ask students: *Which type of word is often unnecessary?* (Adjectives) *Which parts of speech are usually essential?* (Nouns and verbs)

Sentences

- To compose sentences using adjectives, verbs, and nouns for precision, clarity, and impact.

Resources

- "Sentences" Notebook file
- individual whiteboards and pens
- paper and pencils
- printout of page 6 from the "Sentences" Notebook file, one copy per student

Whiteboard tools

- Pen tray
- Eraser
- Select tool
- Highlighter pen
- Delete button
- On-screen Keyboard

Getting Started

Ask students to make sentences using the subjects on page 2 of the "Sentences" Notebook file. Invite some students to say and write their examples on the SMART Board. Go to page 3. Write one of the previous sentences on the board, as a stimulus, and discuss what makes it a sentence. Write a class definition of *sentence*.

Mini-Lesson

1. Say two collections of words. Ask students to decide which collection is a sentence, and write the corresponding letter on their individual whiteboards. For example:

   A. *The dog barked.*　　B. *The broken door*　　(Answer: A)

2. Discuss how students identified which was a sentence.

3. Use the On-screen Keyboard to type some correct sentences onto page 4 of the Notebook file. Through discussion, establish that each sentence is about someone or something (the subject) and an action (the verb). Introduce these terms *subject* and *verb*. Drag the labels out of the boxes "label 1" and "label 2."

4. Circle the subjects and verbs in each sentence with a matching color or highlight the words with the appropriate color.

5. Demonstrate extending the sentence with more information. For example: *The dog barked at the cat.* Ask students in pairs to repeat this for the other sentences.

6. Drag the final label, *ending*, from the box "label 3."

7. Highlight or circle the sentence endings with a matching color.

8. In pairs, ask one student to write a subject, then the other student to write a verb and ending. Write up some of their completed sentences. Repeat, reversing roles.

9. Ask students what is wrong with the short piece of text on page 5. Read the words aloud, with and without an appropriate pause. Ask students: *What can you do to show that there are two sentences here?* Correct the sentences.

Independent Work

Show the text on page 6 of the Notebook file, and give out a copy of the page to each student. Explain that the writer has forgotten to mark the sentences. Read out the text to the class and tell them that they must add the capital letters and periods to their copy of the text. The number of missing periods is hidden in the Hint panel.

Support less-confident learners by using the Eraser from the Pen tray to reveal the hint. Challenge more-confident learners to prepare a similar test for classmates.

Wrap-Up

Ask students to take turns reading parts of the text aloud. Do others agree about how a line is read? Ask volunteers to drag the capital letters and periods to the correct places. Delete the panel on the left to reveal the correctly punctuated version. On page 7, review the main features of a sentence to assess students' learning and review any common misunderstandings. Press the Check features box to confirm.

Verbs

Learning objective

To compose sentences using adjectives, verbs, and nouns for precision, clarity, and impact.

Resources

"Build Your Own" file
"A Mixed Menagerie" (p. 71)

Whiteboard tools

Pen tray
Select tool
Highlighter pen
On-screen Keyboard
Blank Page button
Gallery

Getting Started

Open the "Build Your Own" file on the Main Menu page. This contains a blank Notebook page and a selection of Gallery resources. Remind students of the work on building sentences (p. 40). Ask: *What was needed in each sentence?* (Capital letter, period, subject, verb)

Focus on the verb. Define *verb* as a doing or being word and write this on the SMART Board. A verb can express an action, a happening, a process, or a state. Every sentence needs a verb. Display the picture of a dog (from the English folder under Year 3 in the My Content folder in the Gallery) on the SMART Board and ask for some suitable doing words for the dog (*barked*, *walked*, and so on). Write these words underneath the picture. Repeat for other examples (using, for instance, the images of a boy or a baby from the English folder in the Gallery); no more than two per page.

Mini-Lesson

1. Write the following sentence on the SMART Board: *The dog barked.* Ask students to identify the subject and the verb.

2. Progress to longer sentences, such as: *The kite flew into the air.* Ask a student to identify and highlight the verb.

3. Explain that a verb can be a chain of words. Provide examples such as: *The dog is escaping.* Work together to change the verbs on the board into chains.

4. Discuss how verbs may have similar meanings. Establish that it is important to select the right one for meaning and impact.

5. Encourage students to substitute new verbs in some sentences on the board. Give students prompts, such as: *A verb to express height*—"The kite *soared* into the air."

6. Demonstrate these substitutions on the board by typing or writing over the verbs.

7. Ask a student to cross the room. Write up the sentence: *Harry ___ across the room.*

8. Ask the other students, on individual whiteboards, to write an appropriate verb in the blank (such as *Harry rushed across the room*). Share answers, typing the most appropriate verbs.

9. Repeat the game. Progress to other actions such as *talking*, *looking*, and *writing*. Draw attention to particularly expressive verbs and write them on the board.

Independent Work

Explain that you want students to write a poem on the theme of animals. Tell them that the verbs must be chosen carefully to suit the animals. Ask students to finish the poem on "A Mixed Menagerie" (p. 71). Tell them to treat it as a first draft, which they will try to improve, particularly the verbs, before writing a final version. Support students by helping them with their choice of animal and appropriate verbs. Challenge students to identify verbs in a given text.

Wrap-Up

Invite students to read drafts to the class. Select and praise appropriate verbs. Write these verbs on a new page on the SMART Board and add them to some of the pictures on the board if appropriate. Explain that you are starting a class collection of expressive verbs.

Words Ending in -*ed*

Learning objective

- To compose sentences using tense consistently (present and past).

Resources

- "Words Ending in -*ed*" Notebook file
- "It's in the Past" (p. 72)
- individual whiteboards and pens

Whiteboard tools

- Pen tray
- Select tool
- Highlighter pen
- On-screen Keyboard
- Page sorter

Getting Started

Open the "Words Ending in -*ed*" Notebook file and go to page 2. Invite some students to talk about what they did last night. As they speak, make a list of the verbs they use (such as *walked*, *played*). Ask students if they notice anything that the words have in common. Students should notice that most of the words end in -*ed*. Tell them that this is because these things happened in the past.

Mini-Lesson

1. Explain to students that verbs (action words) change depending on when the action happened. Demonstrate this with an example.

2. Read the six words on page 3 of the Notebook file. Share the rule that these words follow when they are used in the past tense.

3. Ask students to choose one of the words and write it in the past tense on an individual whiteboard.

4. Invite some students to move the orange circle over the words to check their answers. Encourage students to try to verbally put the words into past-tense sentences.

5. Repeat this process with the other rules illustrated on pages 4 to 7.

6. Together, read the present-tense sentences on page 8 and explain to students that their task is to put them into the past tense. Ask them to highlight the verbs in each sentence.

7. Look closely at the highlighted words and consider whether those words need to be changed to put the sentences in the past tense.

8. Double-click on the text and change the correctly highlighted words into the past tense as appropriate using the On-screen Keyboard. Then move the orange rectangle to reveal the correct answers under each sentence.

Independent Work

Give students a copy of "It's in the Past" (p. 72). Ask them to rewrite the sentences in the past tense, as though the action happened yesterday.

Wrap-Up

Ask every student to write a sentence about something he or she did last weekend, ensuring that students write the verb correctly in the past tense. On page 9 of the Notebook file, complete the table of the five rules that a verb can follow in the past tense. For example: add -*ed*; remove the -*e* and add -*ed*. Ask students to look at the verb in their sentence and decide which rule it follows, then ask them to put their verbs in the correct group in the table. Use page 10 to assess whether students understand the rules. Press on the column headings to go to the appropriate pages (3 to 7) to remind students of the rules. Return to page 10 by selecting it in the Page Sorter. Decide on the correct rule for each word and drag the words into the appropriate column.

Past, Present & Future Tenses

earning objective

To compose
sentences using
tenses consistently
(present and past).

esources

"Past, Present &
Future Tenses"
Notebook file
"Past, Present,
Future" (p. 73)
individual white-
boards and pens
pencils
prepared cards
with written
simple actions
that students
could mime (such
as *catch a fish* or
throw a ball)

Whiteboard tools

Pen tray
Select tool
On-screen
Keyboard

Getting Started

Ask a student to stand in front of the class and choose an action card (see Resources). Tell the student to act out the action on the card. Ask one of these questions: *What is he doing now? What did he do yesterday? What will he do tomorrow?* Encourage students to answer in a sentence. For example: *Now he is catching a fish. Yesterday he caught a fish. Tomorrow he will catch a fish.*

Repeat this with a few different action cards. Correct any misconceptions about the use of different tenses. Make a note of the verbs used on page 2 of the "Past, Present & Future Tenses" Notebook file.

Mini-Lesson

1. Explain that action words often change depending on when the actions took place. Refer students back to an example from Getting Started and remind them how the verb changed as the tense changed.

2. Read the sentences on page 3 of the Notebook file. Ask students to talk with a partner to decide which sentence is about what is happening now, which is about what happened in the past, and which is about what will happen in the future.

3. Invite students to share their ideas with the rest of the class and discuss them. Once they have done this, ask volunteers to come to the SMART Board to drag and drop the sentences into the appropriate boxes.

4. Ask: *Do each group of sentences have anything in common?* Encourage answers such as: *All of the future-tense sentences have* will *in them.*

5. Next, go to page 4 and invite students to complete the sentences using the correct tense.

Independent Work

Give each student an enlarged copy of "Past, Present, Future" (p. 73). Discuss what is happening in each picture. Ask students to write three sentences about each picture—one in the past tense, one in the present tense, and one in the future tense. Invite students to sort the sentences into past, present, and future. Ask which words show when the action took place.

Give less-confident learners a selection of sentences written in the past, present, or future tense and read them together.

Wrap-Up

Display page 5 of the Notebook file. Ask each student to pick an action word from the page and to write down, on their individual whiteboards, three sentences containing the action word; one in the past, one in the present, and one in the future tense. Allow students to share some of their sentences and use this opportunity to assess whether they still have any misconceptions about the way verb tenses are formed or used. Finally, move the purple circle around the Notebook page to reveal the correct past and future tense of each verb.

Adjectives

- To make decisions about form and purpose.
- To compose sentences using adjectives for precision, clarity, and impact.

Resources
- "Adjectives" Notebook file
- individual whiteboards and pens
- a collection of different objects (such as colorful toys, little and big objects, colored pencils and crayons) for each group of students

Whiteboard tools
- Pen tray
- Select tool
- Highlighter pen
- Shapes tool
- On-screen Keyboard
- Delete button

Getting Started

Establish the learning objective on page 1 of the "Adjectives" Notebook file. Go to page 2 and ask students to describe the two animals on display. Annotate their suggestions on the page.

Mini-Lesson

1. Look at the collected words together. Ask students if they are all the same type of words. Through questioning, lead them to understand that some words are nouns (such as *animal* or *mammal*), but others are adjectives. Highlight the adjectives.

2. Discuss the term *adjective*. Ask: *What is it? What is it used for?* Annotate students' responses on page 3. Explain that an adjective is a word used to describe somebody or something. Adjectives can be used to describe nouns.

3. Ask students to write a sentence on their whiteboards that uses at least one of the adjectives from page 2. For example: *The elephant is a big and strong animal.* Invite students to read out loud or show their sentences.

4. Go to page 4 and read the sentence out loud. Ask students how they could extend it using adjectives. Write some suggested adjectives around the sentence. Delete the bone at the bottom to reveal one example of the extended sentence.

5. Discuss the benefits of adding adjectives to the text. (The reader learns more.) Ask students for some more examples of sentences with and without adjectives.

6. Play a speaking and listening game. Give each group of students a collection of objects. Have one student use adjectives to describe an object to the rest of the group. The others have to correctly identify the object. Have students take turns.

Independent Work

The next activity on page 5 of the Notebook file emphasizes the value of accurate adjectives. Challenge students to compose short notices for the *Missing!* board. Explain that there is no room for a missing item's photograph, so students will have to think of a detailed description. For example: *It is furry, yellow, and old.* (Teddy bear) Remind them of the importance of using accurate adjectives as they have just done in the game (see Mini-Lesson, above). Students may think of a personal item or use a classroom object if they need visual support. As an extra challenge, ask students to produce computer-written versions of their final work.

Wrap-Up

Listen to and add some of the examples to page 5 of the Notebook file. Use the Shapes tool to add a box in which to write the notices. Identify all the adjectives that have been used. Ask students to think of a notice for the missing dog on page 6. Drag the picture of the dog to one side to reveal the notice. On page 7, summarize what students have learned. Take a vote on the top five most interesting adjectives that have been used in this lesson.

Singular & Plural Nouns

Learning objective

To investigate and identify basic rules for changing the spelling of nouns when *s* is added.

Resources

"Singular & Plural Nouns" Notebook file

"Singular and Plural" (p. 74)

individual whiteboards and pens

Whiteboard tools

Pen tray

Select tool

Highlighter pen

Screen Shade

On-screen Keyboard

Spotlight tool

Getting Started

Show page 2 of the "Singular & Plural Nouns" Notebook file, on which a number of words are given. Ask for suggestions as to how the words can be sorted into two groups. Share ideas. Write and explain the terms *singular* and *plural*. Use these as labels and sort the words into two sets.

Mini-Lesson

1. Read the text on page 3 of the Notebook file. Work with students, identifying and highlighting plural nouns ending in -*s*.

2. Ask students: *What is the total number of plurals in the text?* (19) Pull down the Screen Shade to reveal the highlighted plurals.

3. Explain that the addition of -*s* is the usual way for a noun to change from singular to plural.

4. Go to page 4. Discuss and write the singular forms of the words in the table.

5. Next, ask a student to read aloud a singular form and invite another student to say its plural. Ask: *How many syllables did you hear?* Note that the addition of -*s* does not add another syllable.

6. Now examine some other plural forms. Write the words: *church*, *bench*, and *witch* (which all end in a shushing sound) on page 5. Invite individuals to read one and say its plural. Establish that a new syllable is always added to these words. Write the plurals on the SMART Board and explain that -*es* created the new syllable.

7. Go back to page 3 and activate the Spotlight tool. Set the shape of the spotlight to Rectangular (using the drop-down menu) and focus on the word *cherries*. Discuss the spelling change between the singular and plural forms of the word. Repeat this for the word *knives*.

8. Display page 6 and discuss the spelling patterns for words that end in -*y*. Test examples, such as *play* and *penny*, and write their plural endings. Add some of students' examples onto page 5.

9. Talk about the difficulty with singular words containing *f*: most become -*ves*, but some plurals are -*fs*.

Independent Work

Using the "Singular and Plural" reproducible sheet (p. 74), ask students to sort the words in groups according to how they form their plurals.

Support less-confident learners by concentrating on one or two plural groups. As an extra challenge, ask students to add their own words to the groups.

Wrap-Up

Go to page 7 of the Notebook file. Discuss the singular nouns and ask individuals to say the plural forms. Check the answers by moving each word across the black bar in the center of the screen; the plural version of the word will appear on the other side of the bar. As you reveal the plurals, emphasize the spelling patterns. Discuss any misconceptions that may have arisen.

Conjunctions

Learning objective
• To show relationships of time, reason, and cause through subordination and conjunctions.

Resources
• "Conjunctions" Notebook file
• "Joining Words" (p. 75)
• individual whiteboards and pens

Whiteboard tools
• Pen tray
• Select tool
• Highlighter pen
• On-screen Keyboard
• Page Sorter
• Screen Shade

Getting Started

Show page 2 of the "Conjunctions" Notebook file, which includes the words *and*, *but*, and *or*. Ask students: *What type of words are these?* Use the Eraser to reveal that they are *conjunctions* (joining words). Explain that conjunctions are useful for joining one short sentence to another. Pull the tab to reveal the definition. Remind students about the use of conjunctions and point out that *and*, *but*, and *or* are useful examples, but that we tend to use them too much and forget about other possibilities.

Move on to page 3 and ask students to identify different conjunctions that could be added to the examples. Check students' answers by moving each sentence, in turn, through the rectangle to reveal the completed sentence.

Mini-Lesson

1. Point to some short sentences on notices around the classroom. Ask: *Which pairs of sentences could be joined? What conjunction would you use?* Discourage the use of *and* unless it is the most appropriate choice.

2. Use page 4 of the Notebook file to create a "Conjunctions" word bank that you can keep adding to. Clone some examples from the earlier activities and add them in here if necessary. (Clone words by selecting Clone from the drop-down menu. They can then be moved onto another page by dragging them onto the thumbnail of your destination page in the Page Sorter.)

3. You can save this page into the Gallery to use the words in future lessons. Follow the instructions in the *What to do* section on page 4.

4. Read the narrative text on page 5. Work through the text, one sentence at a time, allowing time for students to think and search for a conjunction.

5. Explain that conjunctions are not always in the middle of the new, longer sentence; sometimes they join at the beginning. Identify examples of this in the text with students. Check that they can identify all of the conjunctions before pulling down the Screen Shade to check.

Independent Work

Introduce the reproducible sheet "Joining Words" (p. 75). Explain that the sheet includes ideas about the school grounds that can be joined together using conjunctions. Show the examples on page 6 of the Notebook file that demonstrate the idea. Focus on each stage of the activity in turn. Invite students to create eight sentences using a conjunction in each sentence. Some helpful conjunctions are presented on the sheet. As an extra challenge, ask students to redo the exercise, using an alternative conjunction each time. Ask them to decide if one choice is more appropriate than the other.

Wrap-Up

Compare answers. Point out that there are many alternatives because more than one conjunction may be appropriate. Write notes on page 7 of the Notebook file, if necessary. Write the preferred sentences on the SMART Board, highlighting the conjunctions. Add these conjunctions to the "Conjunctions" word bank on page 4, adding new pages as required.

Capitalization & Periods

arning objective

To use capital
letters and
periods when
writing
independently.

esources

"Capitalization &
Periods" Notebook
file
"Capital Letters
and Periods"
(p. 76)
pencils

hiteboard tools

Pen tray
Highlighter pen
On-screen
Keyboard
Select tool

Getting Started

Go to page 2 of the "Capitalization & Periods" Notebook file. Introduce the punctuation game to students. Explain to them that they are going to read the text aloud, and when they see a capital letter they must put both hands straight up in the air to make themselves tall like a capital letter; and when they see a period they must stab the air with their index finger as though they are making a period in front of them. Read the text aloud together, combined with the actions.

Mini-Lesson

1. Highlight the capital letters in the text on page 2 of the Notebook file. Ask: *When do we need to use a capital letter?* Remember other uses of capital letters, such as for the beginning of names and for emphasis.

2. Ask: *When do we need to use a period?* Talk about when a new sentence is needed — for example, when the subject of the sentence changes.

3. Show students page 3 and ask them to read it together. Discuss how difficult it is to read correctly without any punctuation.

4. Ask volunteers to come to the SMART Board to add the missing periods and capital letters to the passage. Show them how to double-click on the text and use the On-screen Keyboard to do this.

5. Discuss students' choices with them and address any errors and misconceptions.

6. Demonstrate that reading the sentences aloud makes it possible to hear if the periods and capital letters are placed correctly.

Independent Work

Give each student a copy of "Capital Letters and Periods" (p. 76). Challenge them to rewrite the sentences and the paragraph, putting the capital letters and periods in the correct places — considering all the uses for capital letters. Encourage students to check their work with another student so that discussion and self-evaluation can take place. As an extra challenge, ask students to unjumble the sentences at the bottom of the sheet. Remind them to consider where the capital letter and period should be in each sentence.

Wrap-Up

Display page 4 of the Notebook file. Explain that the sentences have become jumbled. Ask students to consider if there are any clues about the correct order in the words. Suggest that a word beginning with a capital letter needs to go first and that the period will be at the end. Invite individual students to unjumble the sentences on the SMART Board. Challenge students to use capital letters and periods in their independent writing over the next few weeks, and praise evidence of this.

Question Marks

Learning objective

- To use question marks when writing questions.

Resources

- "Question Marks" Notebook file
- prepared cards with a question word on each to support less-confident learners
- individual white-boards and pens
- paper
- pencils
- a cardboard crown (optional)

Whiteboard tools

- Pen tray
- Highlighter pen
- On-screen Keyboard
- Select tool

Getting Started

Open the "Question Marks" Notebook file and read the text on page 2. Ask students to find examples of questions in the text and invite a student to highlight them on the screen. Focus on the question word used at the start of each question.

Ask students to work with a partner on individual whiteboards to make a list of words that might begin a question. Make a class list of question words including *what*, *why*, *who*, and so on.

Mini-Lesson

1. Read page 3 of the Notebook file together and invite students to highlight any question words found in the text.

2. Check together that the question words are at the beginning of a question in each instance.

3. Explain that there is a punctuation mark called a question mark that is used at the end of question sentences to show clearly that it is a question. Show students how to write a question mark.

4. Ask a student to use the On-screen Keyboard to add a question mark to the end of each identified question.

5. Next, ask students to think of a question that the prince might like to ask Cinderella. Invite them to write it down on their individual whiteboards. Share some of the questions as a class and invite a few students to write their questions on page 4.

6. Assess whether students understand how to use a question mark.

Independent Work

Tell students that they are television reporters and they are going to interview the prince about the ball. Encourage them to think about what questions they would like to ask the prince before they begin to write. Invite them to write their list of questions. Remind them about using a question word at the beginning of a question and a question mark at the end.

Provide less-confident learners with a bank of question word cards (see Resources) that can be used to begin a question.

Wrap-Up

Place a cardboard crown on one student's head. Tell the student with the crown that he/she is the prince. Ask one student to read out one of his or her questions to the prince while another student writes the question on page 5 of the Notebook file. Encourage the student playing the prince to try to answer the question in the role of the prince. Assess students' use of question words and question marks during this part of the lesson.

Commas

Learning objective

To use commas to separate items in a list.

Resources

"Commas" Notebook file

"Shopping List" (p. 77), copied onto cardstock and cut apart individual whiteboards and pens

Whiteboard tools

- Pen tray
- Highlighter pen
- On-screen Keyboard
- Select tool

Getting Started

Display page 2 of the "Commas" Notebook file. Give students individual whiteboards and ask them to make a list of their five favorite television programs or their five favorite books. (Write the chosen item on the line.) Look at and compare the different ways in which students present their lists. Some may work down the board and some may work across it. Focus on a list that has been made across the board. Ask: *Are the items in the list clearly separated?* Tell students that you know of something they can use to separate the items in a list.

Mini-Lesson

1. Read the text on page 3 of the Notebook file. Highlight the commas in the two lists and ask students to consider why they are there and what job they are doing.

2. Explain that the commas are used as a substitute for the word *and* in a long list of items. Demonstrate how ridiculous it would sound to keep saying *and* between each item in a long list.

3. Emphasize that the last *and* does not get replaced by a comma.

4. Show students page 4 and ask them if they can identify anywhere that commas could be used.

5. Emphasize how long-winded the lists are with *and* in between each item.

6. Double-click on the text and invite volunteers to use the On-screen Keyboard to replace the extra *ands* with commas.

7. Reread the list with the commas in place and point out how much better it sounds now.

Independent Work

Give each group a set of cards prepared from "Shopping List" (p. 77). Ask students to choose a card to find out what to buy at the supermarket, then write a sentence stating what they bought there. For example: *At the supermarket, I bought an apple, a banana, a toothbrush, a pizza, and some cheese.* Tell students that you are looking for commas separating the items in their lists.

Give less-confident learners a written list with all of the *ands* left in it. Ask them to cross out the *ands* that are not necessary, replacing them with commas.

Wrap-Up

Ask students to explain to a partner how to use commas in lists. Listen to some of the explanations and derive a definitive explanation. Use page 5 of the Notebook file to make a list of ingredients needed for a magic potion. Give students individual whiteboards and challenge them to write their own magic-potion recipe to turn a frog into a prince. Remind them to use commas in their list of ingredients. Once they have done this, invite volunteers to come to the SMART Board to drag and drop the ingredients provided on page 5 into a list. Allow students to share some of their potion ingredients on page 6.

Quotation Marks

Learning objective
- To understand the use of quotation marks and to begin using them in writing.

Resources
- "Quotation Marks" Notebook file
- "What Did She Say?" (p. 78)
- individual whiteboards and pens
- pencils

Whiteboard tools
- Pen tray
- Select tool
- Highlighter pen

Getting Started
Display page 2 of the "Quotation Marks" Notebook file. Tell students that they are going to play the "quotation marks" game. You are going to read the text aloud. When they see an opening quotation mark they must make an imaginary sock puppet open its mouth, and when they see a closing quotation mark they must make it close its mouth. Read the text aloud together and add the actions.

Mini-Lesson
1. Highlight a sentence that is being spoken and highlight the quotation marks at the beginning and the end.

2. Explain that quotation marks are used to show when someone begins to speak (opens their mouth) and when they stop speaking (closes their mouth).

3. Go to page 3 of the Notebook file and ask students to highlight the words that one of the characters is actually saying.

4. Remind students that quotation marks go around the words that are actually being spoken. Invite volunteers to add the missing quotation marks to the text.

5. Look at page 4 and remind students that speech can also be shown in speech bubbles. Ensure that they understand that speech bubbles can be used only where there are pictures of the characters.

6. Provide students with individual whiteboards. Ask them to turn the speech bubbles into story text. For example: *"I am going to meet the Prince," cheered Cinderella.* Invite a couple of students to write their sentences on the SMART Board.

7. Point out the importance of including who is speaking and how they spoke in the sentence.

Independent Work
Give each student a copy of "What Did She Say?" (p. 78). Ask students to underline or highlight all of the words that are actually being spoken by a character, then challenge them to rewrite the sentences with the quotation marks in the correct place. Encourage students to check their work with another student so that discussion and self-evaluation can take place. As an extension, ask students to work in pairs to turn the speech bubbles into story text.

Challenge more-confident learners to work in pairs to write a conversation between Cinderella and the Fairy Godmother. Remind them to show who is speaking and how.

Wrap-Up
Invite two students to write a conversation between Cinderella and the Fairy God-mother using page 5 of the Notebook file. Encourage the other students to check their punctuation, particularly the quotation marks. Encourage students to think of more expressive words than *said* when they are writing who is speaking.

Punctuating Dialogues

Getting Started

Go to page 2 of the "Punctuating Dialogues" Notebook file. Focus on the sentence: *Cinderella said, "Why do I always have to work?"*

Ask students to comment on the punctuation. What is special about it? (Quotation marks separate some words from the rest of the sentence. The quotation marks are used to indicate direct speech.) Reveal the words *direct speech* in the speech bubble and ask for some examples of sentences that include direct speech, either from students' own ideas or taken from a class text. Pull the tab to reveal the definition of the term *direct speech*.

Mini-Lesson

1. Ask students to look in a reading book to investigate the rules for direct speech. Encourage them to make notes on their findings.

2. Display page 3 of the Notebook file and tell students that there are six rules about direct speech. Ask students what they think these are and write their suggestions on the board. Reveal the rules one at a time by dragging the arrows from the bucket of water.

3. Show the excerpt from the story of Cinderella on page 4. Are the rules of direct speech applied? Discuss. Highlight where the rules apply.

4. Invite students to come to the SMART Board and drag the punctuation marks and capital letters into the correct places.

5. Drag down the Screen Shade on the left to reveal the correct punctuation for direct speech.

6. Discuss what each character on page 5 might be saying. Reveal each of the speech bubbles in turn using the Eraser. Point out that speech bubbles are ideal in picture books, but they are not practical in narrative stories.

7. Demonstrate converting a speech bubble into a narrative sentence with direct speech. Look at the example on page 2 of the Notebook file.

8. Invite a student to do this on the board using one of the other speech bubbles on page 5. Check with the class if the rules were followed and repeat for the other two speech bubbles.

Independent Work

Ask students to complete the pictures on "Direct Speech" (p. 79). Each picture needs text to fill a speech bubble. Underneath the boxes ask students to write a narrative sentence with the words inside the speech bubble repeated inside quotation marks. Provide support by asking students to write speech bubbles and supply skeletons of narrative sentences with some punctuation already in place.

Wrap-Up

Add some of the results to the Notebook file on page 6. Emphasize how quotation marks have replaced speech bubbles. Ask students for some more narrative sentences related to the Notebook file.

Apostrophes & Contractions

Learning objective
- To make decisions about form and purpose.

Resources
- "Apostrophes & Contractions" Notebook file
- individual whiteboards and pens
- writing notebooks

Whiteboard tools
- Pen tray
- Select tool
- Highlighter pen
- On-screen Keyboard
- Blank Page button
- Spotlight tool

Getting Started

Read each of the following phrases from page 2 of the "Apostrophes & Contractions" Notebook file in turn: *the pencil of the boy*; *the bags of students*; *the car of the teacher*.

Ask students to work with partners and use them in spoken sentences. Ask: *Is that the way you usually speak?* Discuss how we normally express possession more economically with an *s*, and how in writing, we use an apostrophe. Agree on the short form for each phrase and reveal them.

Mini-Lesson

1. Show the phrases on page 3 of the Notebook file. Continue partner conversations, using these phrases in quick conversations. Encourage natural speech.

2. Invite individuals to write exactly what a partner has said and link it to the complete phrase on the SMART Board.

3. Discuss how the speaker has run words together. Introduce and define the term *contraction*. Pull the definition tab.

4. Emphasize that the missing letter in a contraction needs to be marked by an apostrophe. The Getting Started activity used an apostrophe for possession; a contraction is another use of an apostrophe.

5. Demonstrate and analyze contractions of the other phrases on the board.

6. Move to page 4 and remind students of the story of Cinderella used in earlier lessons. Highlight the apostrophes in the text.

7. Prove that the apostrophes are all being used for contractions by asking students to read a character's words to a partner. Can students speak the words more formally? Discuss and agree on the full versions. Pull the panel across to check answers.

8. Copy and paste or type a list of more difficult contractions onto the table on page 5. Challenge students to provide the full versions of the words on their individual whiteboards. Continue over page 6, if necessary.

Independent Work

Describe the scenario outlined on page 7 of the Notebook file: A robbery has occurred. Two people are being asked for a report: the policeman (trained in making formal reports) and the victim, who speaks and writes more naturally. Two sentences are modeled on page 7. Discuss the differences between the two styles. Ask students to write a report for each character (one formal, one using contractions). Give support by providing phrases for the first report, which will be contracted in the second report. As an extra challenge, ask students to search a picture book for examples of contractions not mentioned in the lesson.

Wrap-Up

Scan the reports onto page 8 of the Notebook file and view, highlighting the contractions. Are apostrophes used correctly? Are there more places where contractions could be used? Add any new contractions to your list on page 6. Create a Contractions word bank for use in future lessons. Add new pages if required.

Long-Vowel Sounds

r _ _ _

s _ _ _ _ _ _

p _ _ _ _

t _ _ _

s _ _ _

t _ _ _

p _ _

w _ _ _ _

p _ _

l _ _ _ _

s _ _

k _ _ _

s _ _ _

r _ _ _

c _ _ _

b _ _

h _ _ _

c _ _ _

m _ _ _

t _ _ _

Joyful Word Search

e	l	c	b	z	j	o	y	g	d
l	y	o	m	a	f	w	c	u	b
o	x	i	n	s	o	i	l	m	o
y	d	n	h	u	s	b	f	v	i
a	t	x	g	a	w	z	e	c	l
l	o	m	f	o	i	l	s	r	t
e	y	t	u	q	p	b	o	y	e
n	s	b	j	m	e	t	p	r	o
i	k	e	r	o	y	a	l	q	d
j	p	o	i	n	t	h	k	v	i

Words

_____

_____

_____

_____

_____

_____

_____

_____

_____

Put some of the words that you have found into sentences.

_____

_____

_____

_____

_____

Write Out the /ou/ Words

Fill in the blanks with words that have the /ou/ sound.

1. The _____ ran back to its hole when it heard the cat meow.

2. "_____!" yelled Kelly, as she stepped on a sharp pebble. "That hurt!"

3. Mom bought a bag of _____ so she can bake cookies later.

4. "_____ do you feel?" Sandra asked Carlos.

5. The funny _____ juggled five balls while riding his unicycle.

6. Did you hear the _____ hooting outside last night?

7. With all my books in it, my bag weighs ten _____.

8. The _____ mooed as the farmer walked by.

9. Those dark _____ look like a storm is coming.

10. Please hang up your wet _____ when you finish taking a bath.

Spelling /âr/ Words

ch<u>air</u>	ch<u>are</u>
c<u>are</u>	c<u>air</u>
f<u>air</u>y	f<u>ea</u>ry
wh<u>ere</u>	wh<u>air</u>
b<u>ear</u>	b<u>air</u>
f<u>air</u>	f<u>ere</u>
th<u>ere</u>	th<u>are</u>
bew<u>are</u>	bew<u>ear</u>
st<u>are</u>	st<u>ear</u>
p<u>ear</u>	p<u>ere</u>

First Crossword

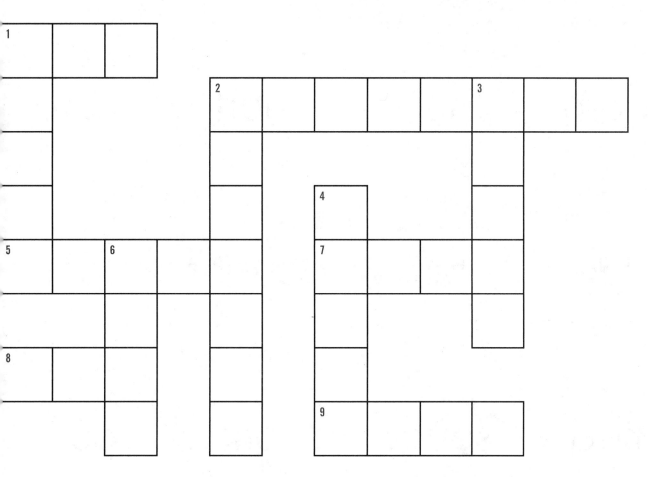

Across

1. Lots of animals have this all over their bodies.

2. The day after Wednesday

5. A fierce wild cat with stripes

7. If you fall over, you could _____ yourself.

8. The opposite of *him*

9. To get water from a faucet you need to _____ it on.

Down

1. If you are the winner of a race, you must have come _____ .

2. If you need a drink, then you are feeling _____ .

3. The opposite of *clean*

4. Something you might wear at school

6. The opposite of *boy*

Sort the Broad /ô/ Words

born	for	short	more
door	turn	caught	floor
bird	sauce	fork	curl
crawl	score	hair	draw
girl	storm	saw	chair

Add a Prefix: *un-* or *dis-*

lucky	agree	available
kind	approve	fair
able	like	comfort
do	honest	happy
cover	appear	bend

Useful Suffixes

Fill in the missing words using the words from the word bank.

WORD BANK	angrily	wonderful	greedily	spoonful	quickly
	playful	kindly	beautiful	carefully	cheerful

1. Shane picked up the glass _____ so he didn't cut himself.

2. Sally looked _____ in her new party clothes.

3. Gran added a _____ of sugar to her tea.

4. The old man shouted _____ at the naughty children.

5. The postman ran _____ because a dog was chasing him.

6. The sun was shining and everyone felt _____ .

7. Tess _____ helped Tim tidy up his toys.

8. The _____ kitten chased the ball of wool.

9. Jill _____ ate all of her candy instead of sharing them.

10. "What a _____ picture," said Zak's teacher.

....

Extra Challenge   Write some more words that end in *-ful* and *-ly* on the back of this sheet.

Antonym Dominoes

left	back	thin	clean	up	rainy
day	happy	push	slow	bumpy	cheerful
night	sad	pull	fast	flat	glum
rough	cold	bottom	freezing	low	quiet
smooth	hot	top	boiling	high	loud
rich	soft	short	small	slim	dry
poor	hard	tall	big	plump	wet
fat	right	front	sunny	dirty	down

Find the Words

Find the hidden words.

investigate	shallowest

greatest	prediction

different	underneath

altogether	clockwise

operation	quadrilateral

Making a Pizza

Cut out each direction and then put them into the correct order. Arrange the directions on a new sheet of paper so that they can be followed easily. Use numbers and arrows to help organize the directions more clearly.

Put the pizza dough onto a plate.

Take the pizza out of the oven and cut it into slices.

Place the pizza on a baking tray and put it in the oven for 20 minutes.

Slice a tomato and lay the slices on top of the cheese.

Grate some cheese and sprinkle it on top of the tomato sauce.

Spread some tomato sauce on top of the pizza dough.

Extra challenge

- Create a set of directions that would explain to an alien how to get ready for school in the morning.

- Remember to use diagrams and arrows as well as words because the alien might not speak any English.

- Remember to think carefully about how you are going to organize your work on the page before you start.

How to Make a Stick Puppet

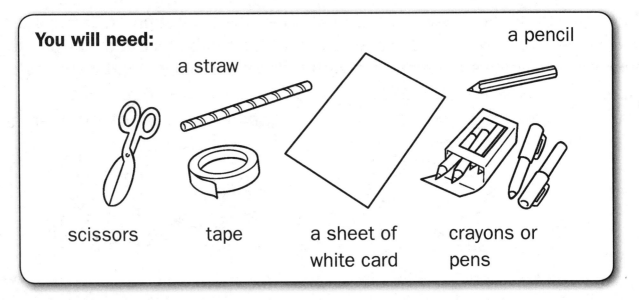

You will need:

a pencil

a straw

scissors   tape   a sheet of   crayons or
                      white card   pens

Method

1. First, choose a favorite character that you would like to make a stick puppet of.

2. Draw the character you have chosen onto a sheet of white card using a pencil. Make sure that the drawing is a sensible size.

3. Color in the drawing using felt-tipped pens or crayons.

4. Carefully cut out the drawing with the scissors. You now have a puppet.

5. Next, place the puppet facedown on the table.

6. Then lay the straw onto the back of the puppet, as shown.

7. Tape the straw to the back of the puppet.

8. Write your name on the back of the puppet.

Story Settings

Everywhere looked white and clean. In the distance were three mountains. Each mountain was covered in snow. A row of green fir trees grew in front of the mountains with their branches covered in snow. In front of the trees, there was a brown log cabin beside a frozen blue lake. Smoke was rising from the chimney of the log cabin. A robin was perched on an old fence post near the lake.

The bedroom carpet was blue. A bed stood in the middle of the room. The quilt cover was red with bright yellow spots on it. Next to the bed was a small bedside table. A clock and a little red book were on the bedside table. A rocking chair stood in the corner of the room and on the rocking chair were three big, brown teddy bears. Hanging from the ceiling of the bedroom were two toy airplanes.

It was a cold and misty night. A full white moon peeped out from behind a cloud. On top of a hill at the end of a long winding path, there stood a haunted castle. The castle was old with a turret at each corner. The windows were broken, and the big wooden door was slightly open. There was an overgrown garden in front of the castle. In the garden were three bare trees and a broken bench.

The town was very busy. Lots of people were hurrying from one shop to another. All of the people were carrying lots of shopping bags. They were all wearing winter clothes because it was cold. There was a candy shop in the town with a bright display of candies in the window. Next door to the sweet shop was a toy store. The toy store had two teddy bears and a train set in the window.

Character Profile

This identity card belongs to _____ _____	Name:
	Address:
	Date of Birth:
	Appearance:
	Occupation:
Official Storyland Resident	Personality:

Write a description of your character using the information that you have included on the identity card to help you. Remember to write in sentences!

_____

_____

_____

_____

_____

The Mystery Grows

The next day Mrs. Bloggs arrived at her normal time. She hoped Mr. Singh would be waiting for her. Unusually, he arrived very late.

"_____ ," moaned Mr. Singh, as he

staggered into the room. "Let _____

_____ ."

"You _____ ," replied Mrs. Bloggs,

looking closely at him, "but _____

_____ ."

"My _____ ," mumbled Mr. Singh,

clutching his face. "It _____ ."

Mrs. Bloggs left the room, and Mr. Singh stayed moaning in a

chair. A few minutes went by.

"Here you are," announced Mrs. Bloggs, when she returned

carrying _____ . "This is _____

_____ ."

Use this space to complete the chapter.

_____

_____

_____

_____

_____

_____

_____

Story Planning in Paragraphs

Where? settings: house; seaside; park; swimming pool;
supermarket

Who? characters: boy; girl; baseball player; lifeguard; cashier

What? objects: ball; bike; life vest; pile of canned food;
inflatable boat

PARAGRAPH PLAN

1 _____

2 _____

3 _____

STORY TITLE

_____

OPENING WORDS OF STORY

_____

_____

_____

_____

Story Planner

Story Title:

Chapter 1:

Chapter 2:

Chapter 3:

Chapter 4:

Essential Words

Rewrite these sentences, shortening them to the number of words suggested in the brackets.

Different teeth have lots of different jobs. (4–5)

_____

The clever incisors cut all the food. (3–4)

_____

The long and sharp canines tear pieces of food. (3–4)

_____

The big molars crush the food very well. (3–5)

_____

The incisors are placed very obviously at the front. (5–7)

_____

The dagger-like canines come next in the mouth. (3–4)

_____

The strong molars sit at the very back. (5–6)

_____

Each and every tooth has strong enamel. (4–5)

_____

The tough enamel protects the tooth well. (4)

_____

The enamel is often weakened by its enemy called plaque. (5–6)

_____

A Mixed Menagerie

What a noisy crowd!

The parrot squawks

The monkey chatters

The _____

_____

_____

What a din of noise!

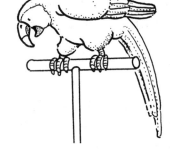

What a greedy gang!

The cat lapped

The _____

_____

_____

What a feast of food!

What an active bunch!

The lion leaps

The snake slides

The _____

_____

_____

What a bustle of movement!

What a _____

_____

_____

_____

_____

What a _____

It's in the Past

Rewrite these sentences in the past tense.

1. Kara eats a snack before doing her homework.

_____

2. Brandon plays soccer with his friends.

_____

3. The car turns right at the corner.

_____

4. The dog chases a squirrel in the yard.

_____

5. Jose finishes his project in time for dinner.

_____

6. Dad buys milk on his way home.

_____

7. The baby falls asleep in his crib.

_____

8. Sammy reads his book in the living room.

_____

9. I help my little sister put away her toys.

_____

10. We watch TV after we finish our homework.

_____

Past, Present, Future

Past	Past
Now	Now
Future	Future
Past	Past
Now	Now
Future	Future
Past	Past
Now	Now
Future	Future

Singular and Plural

Write the plural forms of these words and place them in the correct groups.
Each group needs five words.

puppy	shoe	daisy	watch	book
school	thief	donkey	glass	leaf
fox	match	scarf	tick	key
city	party	shelf	berry	sandwich
day	monkey	bean	toy	wolf

+s	+es	y̶ ies	ys	f̶ ves

Joining Words

Choose a conjunction to join each pair of sentences. Remember to use only one capital letter and one period.

while	so	because	but	if
and	although	until	since	though
before	after	when	that	as

Everyone can enjoy school grounds.
There is plenty to do.

_____

_____

The grounds are complete.
They have been planned.

_____

_____

Climbing equipment is fun.
It can lead to accidents.

_____

_____

A climbing trail should be on grass.
No one gets hurt.

_____

_____

Quiet areas are set aside.
Children can talk quietly.

_____

_____

Some children play ball.
Others chat to friends.

_____

_____

There must be benches.
People can rest.

_____

_____

Baseballs must be banned.
They are too hard.

_____

_____

Capital Letters and Periods

- Put the capital letters and periods in the correct places.

the ugly sisters were very unkind to cinderella

a mouse lived in the corner of the kitchen

on monday morning the ugly sisters told cinderella to clean the kitchen

- Add the missing capital letters and periods.

cinderella was very sad she wanted to go to the ball with her sisters the ugly sisters laughed at cinderella they did not want her to go to the ball the ugly sisters gave cinderella lots of horrible jobs to do on monday she had to clean the kitchen on tuesday morning cinderella had to do the laundry on wednesday afternoon she had to make dresses for the ugly sisters on thursday cinderella had to go shopping by friday she was very tired and very weepy

- Reorder these mixed-up sentences. Use the capital letters and periods to help you.

wanted ball. to go Cinderella the to

_____

sisters The were unkind ugly Cinderella. to

_____

little mouse for felt Cinderella. sorry The

_____

Shopping List

What Did She Say?

• Underline the words that are being spoken, then put the quotation marks in the correct places.

I wish I could go to the ball, sighed Cinderella.

You can go to the ball, replied the Fairy Godmother as she waved her magic wand.

What a beautiful dress, gasped Cinderella happily.

You must be home by midnight, ordered the Fairy Godmother.

• Turn the speech bubbles into a conversation.

_____

_____

_____

_____

_____

Direct Speech

Cinderella

Ugly Sister

Fairy Godmother

Cat

Ugly Sister

The Prince

Notes